SEEN, HEARD, AND PAID

SEEN, HEARD, AND PAID

The New Work Rules for the Marginalized

ALAN HENRY

RODALE

NEW YORK

Copyright © 2022 by Alan Henry

All rights reserved.
Published in the United States by Rodale Books, an imprint of the Crown
Publishing Group, a division of Penguin Random House LLC, New York.
RodaleBooks.com
RandomHouseBooks.com

RODALE and the Plant colophon are registered trademarks of Penguin
Random House LLC.

Library of Congress Cataloging-in-Publication Data has been applied for.

ISBN 978-0-593-23335-1
Ebook ISBN 978-0-593-23336-8

Printed in the United States of America

Jacket design by Anna Bauer Carr

10 9 8 7 6 5 4 3 2 1

First Edition

CONTENTS

SEEN, HEARD, AND PAID

INTRODUCTION

S een, heard, and paid. It's what we all hope for when we start a new job. But for marginalized workers, a group I count myself part of, it often feels like an unattainable goal. When I began at what I imagined would be my dream job, as an editor at the *New York Times*, I thought this would be that moment when I would finally overcome the boundaries of privilege and have access to what should be these three basic worker rights. But I clearly remember the moment when I realized that even at a liberal bastion like the *Times*, it was too much to hope for. I was sitting in a meeting, the purpose of which was to kick off a new initiative in partnership with another group in the newsroom. My team colleagues and I had just introduced ourselves and explained what our roles were and what we did on a daily basis to keep the team moving forward. We talked about our responsibilities and how we all worked together. Overall it was fine, until a colleague showed up late. Because he came in at the tail end of the introductions, everyone stopped and our manager introduced him and told him to fill in the other team on what he did. Without dropping a beat, he proceeded to describe himself as the person responsible for all the work that I had just said that I did, and not as my peer, but as my manager, something that everyone in the room knew was explicitly untrue. Imagine it: If a peer on your team, who is less experienced than you are but is known for being louder, walked in after you had just explained the roles and responsibilities of your job and then claimed to do not only what they actually do but also what you do, and then claimed to essentially be your supervisor, you would probably be livid. And yeah, I was. I stared daggers at our manager, hoping that she would step up and correct the record or at least point out that we worked *together*, but she did no such thing. I looked around the rest of the room, all white faces, and realized that no one was going to help out on my behalf. I got some side glances, especially from the people on the other team who could tell exactly what was happening, but my own teammates were not going to back me up.

Now I had two choices: I could speak up on my own behalf or keep quiet. If I spoke up, I knew I'd come across as an aggressive, angry Black man in a room full of white men and women, some of whom had already proven to me that they weren't particularly interested in my voice, opinions, work, or experience, anyway.

If I stayed quiet, I'd bury all those feelings of being walked on, ignored, and openly disrespected way down deep, where all the other moments of previous marginalization were kept. And that was what I chose. But I regret keeping my silence in that room and having to suck it up as I did. I wish I had the tools then to find a way to speak up either in that room or later with my manager, but I opted for the safe route instead. And sadly, silence is often viewed as compliance.

To get to that moment of crystal clear, blatant marginalization, I had worked in many office settings that had offered their own rules on how to work around both people's prejudices and those of the institutions. First, it was while I was doing IT—mostly support, helping people fix their computers and work more efficiently. Then I went to grad school, earned a business degree, and got a new job and, with it, a promotion to a new world of responsibilities: project management. I worked as a project manager long enough to learn how to handle multiple projects and demanding clients and how to help my colleagues do their best work when everything was on fire and everything was high priority. I thank a rather high-maintenance and high-energy chief information officer (CIO) for those skills, to be honest. Working for him was both frustrating and empowering. I learned a ton and eventually turned what was then my side hustle—tech journalism—into a full-time job, and I brought those skills with me.

Tech journalism was a new world that was full of some of the same pressures (How many stories can we file this week? Will we meet our deadlines? How do we organize all our editorial priorities?) but with different people and a different audience, many of whom desperately needed help with the same kinds of situations I'd muddled through in my career in technology. So I started to tackle and blend two of my favorite topics—productivity and technology—and it just so happened I landed at an outlet that traded in that kind of advice: *Lifehacker.*

From there I learned entirely too much about the world of productivity and its role in helping people work smarter, get more done, and achieve their career goals. I wrote article after article teaching readers how to get things done, how to enjoy their lives more, and how to make their lives better and healthier. It was all great work, and I'm proud of it, but I didn't realize at the time that much of the advice that resonated so much with our audience was written by and for people who may have needed it the least.

To be fair, everyone can use help getting their work done faster so they can spend more time doing what they want to do, but marginalized people—people whose contributions are often overlooked in their workplaces because of their race, their gender, their sexuality, or their gender expression—need that advice more than others do, and often that advice doesn't speak to them at all. To be productive, we need to be seen, heard, and paid fairly for our work. Affording these rights to everyone requires a new look at how work is done and a new set of real-world work rules for people who are sidelined and who lack privilege.

I tried to make changes in that direction at *Lifehacker*, but by the time the site had changed ownership and management, it was clear that this more inclusive focus wasn't the direction the group wanted to go. I took my message to the *Times* and did have success getting the word out. There I found an amazing platform to help people and met great friends who were supportive. However, it was at that same hallowed institution that I really learned what it meant to be marginalized. (I talk a lot about my experiences at the *Times* in this book. A lot. It's not to demonize the company or the many wonderful people who work there. But if this institution that is known as a beacon of shining light on the darkness in this world can also be a harbor of all that is wrong with marginalizing employees, then think of how insidious this culture is throughout all workplaces.)

Today, I've been writing about productivity for the better part of a decade. I get up in the morning with the hope that something I've written will help someone improve their life. But when I realized that some of the same tips and techniques that I wrote about didn't work in my own life—and didn't work as well for people who were more like me than unlike me—I started to wonder why.

After all, if I block off my calendar for a whole day, calling it

No-Meeting Tuesdays, at best my colleagues would laugh and schedule me for meetings anyway, because Tuesday was more convenient for them. At worst, they'd question me, challenge me, dare me to even assert the right to manage my own time when they wanted it instead. When I took a position where I had a colleague who not only did the same thing and was praised for it but also would actively decline and reject meeting requests for his no-meeting day, some of the differences started to come into view.

My awareness of these differences doesn't mean that I'm not shaken when I face discrimination or marginalization in the workplace. Nor does it mean that it's not a heavy emotional and psychological toll to carry. But people of color, women, LGBTQ+ folks, and any other marginalized group at work have to carry it every day.

You carry it with you when you walk into a new workplace. You carry it with you when you meet a new team or when you stand up to lead a meeting. You carry it with you whenever you meet a new client or take on a new project. And it doesn't matter—despite what some people say—how good your work is or how talented you are. The social baggage can, and does, have an impact.

I hope that in these pages, I can offer those of you who face these challenges a new approach to work, along with perhaps a bit of solace in knowing that, first, you're not alone—certainly not as alone as you feel. Second, there are things you can do to make yourself feel empowered at work and to take some measure of control back from the forces around you—forces that are, by their very design, meant to make you feel less qualified, less valuable, and less talented than your colleagues.

For those of you who lead and manage others, I hope that here you'll find a wealth of experiences that, while they may not match your own, you can respect and appreciate as things that your colleagues bring with them to work every day. I hope that you can begin to unpack the biases and systems that, in your own workplace and on your own teams, contribute to marginalization in the workplace.

THE PARADOX OF PRODUCTIVITY

If your manager hired you, this person probably had at some moment decided that you were the best candidate for the position or, at the very least, a good fit for the job. So your manager should be expecting and encouraging your most productive work. But for marginalized workers, that encouragement often doesn't materialize. Much of this book is about how to be productive within the system and with the built-in biases of your boss. But your job is not to educate your workplace on discrimination or come up with a wholesale fix for racism. And that's not what this book is about, either. Your job is to be a superstar, to get to the glamour work—not the office housework—and to find ways to spend less time on the things you have to do so you can spend more time on the things you want to do. And that's what this book is here to help you with.

RULE 1

Inclusion Only Works
If Everyone Buys In

(BEING MARGINALIZED)

The first rule of being seen, heard, and paid starts with understanding if you are being marginalized. For the sake of clarity, I'll dispense with a few formalities right here. First of all, I'm not going to spend time proving to you that people of color, members of the LGBTQ+ community, women, people with disabilities, and other minority groups of all stripes, whether they're ethnic minorities, religious minorities, or just underrepresented in their field or workplace, suffer specific challenges when they go to work every day. Or that the challenges compound if their identities intersect with any of those labels, especially in a way they can't or won't consciously hide or minimize when they go to work. Those people bring with them a level of social baggage that they can't leave behind or just sideline and hope they have a nice day at the office. (Well, in truth, most of us do just that—we put it in the backs of our minds and hope against hope that we won't have to deal with microaggressions today, or that our colleagues, even if they're well-meaning, don't say something offensive.) Our majority counterparts—and yes, that means white, male, cisgender, and heterosexual in most workplaces—don't have to bring those same concerns to work. One person's well-meaning curiosity can be another's oppressive straw on our backs while we're all trying to do our best at the office. If you have issues with that basic thesis, then there's a whole world of data to back up what I'm saying. Google it and don't engage in bad faith, and you'll learn a lot. This isn't a book about marginalization, or proving that it exists—it's a book about how to succeed at work regardless of your identity, and especially if your identity is one that's in the minority.

MARGINALIZED DOESN'T MEAN WHAT YOU THINK IT DOES

What does marginalized mean to you? Sure, Black workers can be marginalized in majority-white workplaces, as I have been. However, white workers (especially white women) can also be marginalized in spaces where they're the minority. The differences, of course, come down to both organizational and social power dynamics. Strictly, to be marginalized means you're a member of a social group that has been traditionally kept out of, or away from, power, decision-making, or import and that you are consequently treated as insignificant or somehow less than those who make up the majority or the empowered people. In an office setting, being marginalized can mean being kept from power and decision-making, but it can also mean simply being excluded from the greater culture that permeates the space.

To illustrate the point a bit further, I spoke with Ruchika Tulshyan, CEO and founder of Candour, a diversity and inclusion strategy firm that works with organizations to root out these kinds of biases. The company trains employees on antiracist behaviors that help marginalized or minority employees stand on even ground with their majority, privileged colleagues. I initially met and spoke with Tulshyan while writing a piece for the *New York Times* about how to find success if you've been discriminated against or marginalized at work—a piece largely based on my own experiences there.[1] I knew I had been marginalized, but aside from knowing how it feels, how do you describe that to someone else? "Long-standing research on tokenism," she said, citing research that Rosabeth Moss Kanter conducted in the 1970s at Harvard Business School, "has shown that when you're the only or one of the few of a historically underrepresented group in a work environment, it can have a profound impact on your workplace experience. You can face increased scrutiny and pressure to conform to a stereotype. You may struggle to find role models or even models of success that look like you."

At the *Times,* I worked with some of the smartest, most talented people I'd ever met. The environment, however, definitely had its arrangement of social circles, some more difficult to penetrate than others, especially if it was your job to try to work your way into them. My role there was supposed to be a bit of a liaison across multiple areas of the newsroom, kind of preaching the gospel of service journalism (as in journalism intended to inform and provide actionable advice and useful context to the news of the day to readers) to journalists who may not have thought that this was their realm of expertise or their responsibility to consider. I was successful in some spaces, but in others, I clearly wasn't welcome.

I don't attribute the tepid reception I received to my ethnicity or the combination of my ethnicity and gender (or my physical appearance at all, frankly), but privilege has many levels, like Dante's *Inferno*. Where you did or didn't go to school or how much money you have or the path you took to that particular job can be just as important or damning as the color of your skin. And yes, some people, even at the *Times*, still think you're not a real journalist if you didn't graduate from a certain prestigious school in Boston and then work for years at local newspapers before "graduating" to "the Paper." It's unfortunate, but as much as I thought walking into the organization having previously been an editor in chief of a popular publication and having a decade of writing and editing experience under my belt would make a difference, it didn't. Being willing to learn and eager to talk and share ideas with people who had more experience than I did didn't matter, either. Was it any less painful to feel sidelined because of my background and not just because I was one of the few Black men in the newsroom? No, it wasn't. And there were plenty of moments I also felt marginalized for that, too.

"It's enraging that the burden of proof of racism is put on the marginalized, not the perpetrator," Tulshyan told me. "As a society, we need more empathy that being the only one, or one of the few, puts immense pressure on people in majority-white organizations. Coupled with the fact that three-quarters of white Americans don't have a single friend of color, it's not hard to imagine that white employees who may initially face some exclusion (because they're new/junior, etc.) will still likely find themselves later accepted or, at the very least, find other white people (even if not on their immediate team) to build alliances with.[2] This is very, very hard for people of color who are the numerical minority."

I also asked Tulshyan about the social baggage that marginalized workers bring into the office every day without necessarily wanting to. For example, I asked her, what about the white employee who wouldn't think that describing a Latinx woman on the same team as "fiery" but who is indeed marginalizing her? Those behaviors, while simultaneously deniable and simply cliquish, are actually harmful. Tulshyan agreed. "One of the big issues (and harder to track but absolutely key)," she said, "is that these discriminatory behaviors end up having an implicit or overt impact on a person of color's career progression. When this hypothetical person is seen as 'fiery,' her manager may think she isn't deserving of a pay raise or advancement. That also casts a long shadow on how other Latinx team members are viewed."

The wider implications of marginalization explain why it matters more than just not having someone to eat lunch with and why it so often takes many forms. Sometimes it's simply about being the only person or one of a few people like you in a space, regardless of your background. Yes, sometimes being marginalized takes a clear form, such as being discriminated against openly because you're a woman in a predominantly male workplace, or being passed over because some manager thinks you may start a family soon and therefore shouldn't be given more responsibilities if you're just going to leave the company. Being marginalized can also look like not being invited out for dinner with the team or for drinks ever, merely because you're not one of the "cool kids." It can also come in the shape of a pay gap between women and men in similar jobs, or between white employees and employees of color. It can look like a white employee's getting promoted simply because a minority employee with a more senior role joined the team. Tulshyan elaborated: "Shonda Rhimes calls it FOD. Being the first, only, or different. She writes in her book, *Year of Yes,* about how being an

FOD can make it feel like you have to represent your whole group in every interaction—your success is not yours alone, as in you're fighting a stereotype, and that pressure of if you fail and let down your whole community is real."

Being marginalized usually shows itself in those smaller, more insidious forms, where one person may mean the slight but no one else does. Or it's innocent enough to ignore if you don't want to rock the boat (like when all the other team members avoid talking about the person whom none of them invited to drinks on a given night). These episodes of marginalization are often deniable or even excusable. They are designed to make the person being marginalized spend more time thinking about whether something is actually happening. They wind up spending more energy trying to work around their feelings and the intentions of the offender than they spend working and succeeding at their actual jobs. In my case, being marginalized meant being removed from passion projects in favor of less qualified people at one job. At another job, it meant being sidelined and having my ideas and work stolen and executed by others, who then took credit for them and their subsequent success, even after I'd departed. Marginalization comes in large and small ways, but it's always an emotional toll that you should be aware of whenever you walk into a space where you're a minority.

EVERYONE'S VOICE HAS TO MATTER

Cliques exist for a reason: to keep a certain kind of person out and other people in. But here's the thing about cliques in the workplace. They don't *have* to exist. When they exist, there's usually a more nefarious cause at their root, according to Meghan French Dunbar, cofounder of Conscious Company Media and the podcast *World-Changing Women*. "That to me is an absence of leadership and an absence of vision of how the workplace is supposed to be," she told me when I explained how cliquish some of the offices I've worked in were. She pointed the finger squarely at company managers and other leaders for allowing cliques to develop and to marginalize team members whom the clique doesn't approve of. When I asked her more about the role that management—even middle managers—plays at creating inclusive, collaborative environments, she explained further: "It's not necessarily corporate values that you laminate and slap up on a wall. It's about how those [values are] lived and expressed through the leadership, and how that has permeated the entire culture itself."

"This is something that we did at my company," Dunbar continued. "We actually brought every single stakeholder—that was every employee, every team member—to the table to come up with our corporate values, to redefine our corporate values together as an organization. As a part of that process, we literally said, 'Everybody's voice here matters. We need to come to a consensus as an organization, what our values are moving forward, and what does it look like for us to embody these?'"

"It is incumbent upon you as the leader to step up and come up with some foundational process, to bring everybody to the table," Dunbar explained. In short, it's up to managers to not just outline the values they want on their teams but also to live them and act them out continually—to do the things necessary for marginalized employees to feel included. It's part of management, and no productivity tip or hack will change that. But managers must also check in with their teams regularly to make sure they're embodying the behavior the managers want to see. Dunbar explained the benefit of this approach: "That, hopefully, gives those who are feeling marginalized and left out of place to say, like, 'I didn't feel like we were living up to our corporate values last week when I wasn't invited to this meeting.'"

Of course, in the absence of good managers, you can always take it on yourself to attempt to break into a clique that you're trying to be a part of, but it's a big ask for anyone. And it's much like having to take on a second job to try to level up in your career or even just have workplace friends. Even if you're successful, you have to contend with all the reasons you were excluded in the first place. If you've been excluded because of your race, ethnicity, gender, sexuality, or religion, it's really not worth trying to join that clique.

FORGE YOUR BONDS WITH PEOPLE WHO CAN SUPPORT YOU, AND DOCUMENT EVERYTHING

So other than just feeling awful, as I often did, sitting alone in the office or finding places to work that were semipublic but still lonely, what do you do if you're the marginalized person at work? Much of this book is about overcoming different elements of being sidelined. But there are a few key big-picture things that you can do to find some mental stability without letting your exclusion get under your skin.

"First, know you are not to blame," Tulshyan said. "It's not your problem to fix, and sadly, you're not alone. My first piece of advice is actually to find others you can talk to at the organization, if possible. Are there people of color in other departments you could connect with? Other employees from other marginalized backgrounds? Ensure you enlist some backup. Then, I would say, assess the best way to approach the situation—can you talk to your manager? To a colleague in the majority who could be an active bystander? To HR? What is the best approach that suits the culture of this organization? Document instances of exclusion, no matter how slight they may seem. It's important to be able to demonstrate a pattern, not one-off incidents. Most of all, as I always say, if you find you are not welcome and valued and that there isn't going to be support to ensure you thrive, it may be important for your health and sanity to walk away."

In most situations where I felt marginalized, I found value in working around the people who I felt were marginalizing me. On a few occasions, I chose to develop a closer working relationship with my direct manager, who was happy to chat with me more often and discuss how I could make my ideas work without necessarily including the team members who pushed me to the side. On another occasion, I focused instead on forming a cohesive team that was willing to do its best work for our collective benefit, rather than pleasing any given person at the top of the chain. Whatever your approach, the core message is the same: Spend your time and energy on the people who value your time and who value you, not the people who don't and won't.

Going back to my stint at the *Times,* I found much solace in joining employee resource groups, or ERGs. We had groups for many different people and identities, and you could join as many or as few ERGs as you chose to. I was a proud member of Black@ NYT, the ERG for Black employees, and we had regular meetings and events just to connect with each other and to share our experiences. At professional events our Black@NYT held with other media companies' ERGs, we could network professionally and inform each other about job opportunities or just make friends with other people who shared similar lived experiences. ERGs aren't specific to journalism or media companies, either—many large companies of all types have employee groups for people with specific ethnicities, religions, disabilities, gender representations, or sexualities. Seek them out; you'll more often than not find welcoming faces and people who are willing to let you in without forcing you to prove your worth, as other cliques may do.

However, being a member of an ERG like that doesn't change the treatment you get on your own team or from your own manager. Consider these groups a place for venting and safety only if you actually know that it's a safe space for you to share your experiences. The last thing you'd want is to vent about a problematic colleague, only to have someone else in the ERG go tell this individual that you complained.

Additionally, consider industry-wide professional organizations and communities that can help you when things get tough and will support you across specific companies or jobs. I'm not exaggerating when I say that one community of journalists of color saved my life when I joined. I was severely depressed and debating my career in journalism entirely, thinking about whether I wanted to leave and go back to being a project manager. I had felt as if my career had peaked, and while I had a coveted position, I was supremely unhappy and felt isolated. Joining their community gave me a bit of a second home—someplace I could vent freely about my frustrations and get constructive feedback and even a place where I could be called out when I complained unfairly about other people. It's a community that regularly shares job opportunities for those looking to move from one place to another or to take another step in their careers, and community members congratulate one another for their successes and support one another through their failures and setbacks.

Everyone should have a community like it to turn to during their dark moments, and I urge you to seek one out for yourself, whatever industry or field you may be in. Sometimes it might be a labor union or an organization that certifies professionals in your field. When I was a freelance writer, I joined the Freelancers Union long before I worked in a place where I could join the Writers Guild of America or the NewsGuild. And even then, I was eager to join the National Association of Black Journalists. When I was a project manager working in technology, it was the Project Management Institute. There's always an organization that is focused on helping people in a given career but is not tied to a specific job or company. And usually inside or peripheral to that organization, there are additional groups dedicated to the challenges that specific marginalized groups face.

DIVERSITY IS GREAT, BUT IT DOESN'T FIX MARGINALIZATION

And don't think that the fix is to just go work for a company or an organization that takes diversity and representation seriously. After all, you may find yourself in a space where there are plenty of people like you but where you're marginalized for other reasons, as I mentioned earlier. Maybe it's not your skin color but it's where you went to college. Maybe it's not your gender or sexuality but it's what part of town you live in and therefore your class or upbringing. Tulshyan explained that diversity and inclusion are important steps to reducing the reasons why people are marginalized, but they're not a panacea for companies or employees: "It's extremely positive for a team to have as much diversity as possible . . . but extremely negative when marginalized employees feel excluded and devalued," she explained. Describing my own life in a way that was almost uncanny, she elaborated: "It can impact their performance, their engagement and absolutely impact their mental health. When marginalized employees face discrimination, they often feel like they can't speak up, contribute, or take risks, all key markers of feeling psychologically unsafe."

And it's not just the individual who suffers here. When you're marginalized, you don't have a method to bring your best work with you every day, and your employer misses out on everything you have to offer. But it's important to remember that you have a lot to offer. "Sadly," Tulshyan said, "organizational innovation and growth require employees to be able to speak up, so it's a lose-lose for the organization and the marginalized employee. It can have a tremendously negative impact on the marginalized person, and I've now met and interviewed far too many people who have suffered long-term trauma, even severe depression, as a result of facing discrimination and marginalization at work."

Even "Positive" Stereotypes Have Negative Impact

(MICROAGGRESSIONS)

Those with privilege may think *Exclusion* (with a capital *E*) went away with the end of separate-but-equal statutes. But the rest of us know that both large-scale social exclusion and the equally insidious small-scale, individual exclusion (with a lowercase *e*) absolutely still exist and keep us from true equality. I was fortunate to have a pretty inclusive experience during my high school years. Up until then, we had moved around a lot because my dad was in the military. During my elementary and middle school years, I struggled with teachers who preferred to think I was incapable of learning, instead of understanding that I was transferring from schools with different curricula. I regularly had to prove that I could keep up, while my most mediocre classmates would sail past their failing test scores to passing grades. But my high school years were a bright spot. We landed in a diverse, middle-class community in central Maryland. And for the first time, I felt supported and seen.

However, one common refrain I heard during those years was that I was "so articulate" and so "well spoken." These were usually well-meaning white adults, and at the time, I simply took it as a compliment. I didn't know of their comments as anything else, but their words hid a dirty little secret: namely, that they didn't *expect* me to be so well spoken or to speak clearly in a voice that didn't ring with the inflection of African American Vernacular English, or AAVE. If you've ever heard Black Americans speak, you've probably heard some variety of AAVE. But if you were to listen to me speak, you might not, depending on who you are.

The flip side of that same coin came from some of my Black classmates who heard me speak and told me that I talked like a white person. They regularly accused me of being an "Oreo" or trying to "act white." While the comments from my Black classmates were blatantly more insulting and were designed to remind me that I'm an other—both to my Black peers and to my white ones—the comments about my articulateness were just as insidious. They revealed that those white teachers and other adults expected something of me entirely because of my ethnicity, and although they probably had no intention of being racist about it, they were surprised when I was more like them than I was like the other image they had expected me to be.

As a teenager and later as a college student at the University of Maryland, I didn't think much of this. I took it as the compliment that those teachers probably meant it to be, backhanded as it was, and moved on, proud of my ability to communicate clearly when I needed to. As I got older, I realized the importance of being able to navigate multiple spaces—switching my manner of speech and mannerisms depending on my audience or my environment, mostly to communicate to others around me that no, I'm not an *other* that you need to be concerned about. But going back to my younger years, those teachers may or may not have realized that they were saying something distinctly racist or engaging in racist behavior. Either way, that type of behavior is called a *microaggression,* a term originally coined in the 1970s by Harvard psychiatrist Chester M. Pierce and studied in detail by Derald Wing Sue, a professor of counseling psychology at Columbia University, and discussed in his book *Microaggressions in Everyday Life: Race, Gender, and Sexual Orientation.*[1]

Microaggressions are subtle, deniable actions that undermine a person or exclude or malign the individual. The actions are easily explained away by forgetfulness, ignorance, or anything but the malice that often inspires them. Perhaps a more blatant and specific example comes from my friend and colleague Hahna Yoon, who wrote a guide on how to deal with microaggressions for the *New York Times* (full disclosure: I was her editor on the piece).[2] Yoon opens the piece by describing the time a friend's boyfriend went out of his way to explain the concept and history of American Thanksgiving to her, as though she hadn't been raised in the United States. She shared her experiences with online dating and being regularly approached by men who claim to love Asian women almost as a fetish, as though her entire self had been reduced to her ethnicity. We could, as she explains, sit and argue over whether those people meant anything harmful by their actions. We could even discuss whether their actions are racist (they are) or whether their actions make those people racist (unclear, but that's not the point). The point is that the actions are born from racial ignorance and result in behavior that's actively harmful to the person it's inflicted on.

Ironically for an article about microaggressions, not long after we published Yoon's story, a senior editor at the *Times*, a white woman, dashed off a request to the home-page editors—not me or any of the other editors who worked on the story—asking us to pull it down from the home page and to stop promoting it. Before that could happen, though, I got word of her request (largely because for the piece to come down, I'd have to do it myself), and I asked why the editor wanted it removed. It was "not in line with the current news cycle," she responded, through the original person who got the first message. Not wanting to press the matter further or, worse, not wanting to spend whatever political capital I had at that moment, I obliged. At first, I was just frustrated that a great story was being buried for what seemed to be silly reasons. There were no news events that should have forced us to take the story down, and our section of the home page was designed specifically for our kinds of stories. The kinds of journalism that our project produced was, by definition, not always in line with the news cycle. We produced stories that were designed to help improve people's lives and to be relatively evergreen—or useful regardless of when they're read. And this was absolutely one of those stories. Still, I had, up until that point, considered the editor in question a good friend and a colleague, so I decided against pressing the matter any further. Not much later, when sharing the story with others, I learned that the article had struck a nerve with the editor, who had reportedly complicated feelings about microaggressions and whether they were as real and as concerning as we made them out to be in the article.

I never did ask that editor if there was some other reason she didn't like the piece or if there was some editorial reason she didn't want it on the home page. But because she never felt the need to clarify and saw no privilege inherent in her demand (apart from the privilege of her position, of course), we'll never know.

MICROAGGRESSIONS ARE SO INSIDIOUS BECAUSE THEY ARE HARD TO PIN DOWN

Their fleeting nature is key to why microaggressions are so difficult to pin down, examine, and respond to. People who face microaggressions struggle to find the right way to respond to them, because—and this is part of the malice—responding directly or overtly can be perceived as flying off the handle or playing into negative stereotypes of "bitchy" women workers or "angry Black" workers or cultural stereotypes where someone may not understand the subtleties of how badly they've been treated. Instead of focusing on the action and how the action was hurtful, the focus shifts immediately back to the intention of the perpetrator and whether that person meant to do harm, bypassing the need for apology or self-reflection on their part, entirely. In short, the man who approaches Yoon on a dating site and says "Wow, I love Asian women! Do you want to go out sometime?" may think he's being flirtatious and approachable, but instead he has reduced Yoon's entire self to the way he perceives her ethnicity as a tangible thing to be desired and obtained. He may not understand that this behavior is exploitative and racist, but it is. He may not have intended it to be this way, but that doesn't change the fact that it is. And because he is opening with this microaggression, Yoon then has to either ignore it entirely or confront him on his behavior.

WHEN A COMPLIMENT IS NOT A COMPLIMENT

The stereotypes that other people have of us—even when the notions are supposedly positive—follow us around like a cloud over our heads. We can never really shake ourselves free of them, and even in the most "woke" and progressive spaces, they can rear their ugly heads. When a colleague in one of my early journalism jobs was dumbfounded that I didn't follow professional sports or even play a sport myself, he wasn't just surprised that a colleague didn't share a passion for basketball. He *assumed* that I loved basketball and had a history of playing basketball because I'm Black. When I replied that not all Black people play basketball, he naturally went on the defensive and exclaimed that he didn't mean it *that way.* And he probably didn't—but the social baggage that I have to carry, and the social programming he has received his entire life, said otherwise. Now imagine if that same person were a supervisor or a manager, and the person's perception of me actually mattered when it came to my career advancement. I'd be at the mercy of this supervisor's reaction if I chose to call the person out on the stereotype. I'd be more likely to simply let the whole thing slide without acknowledging that the assumption wasn't just wrong but was also hurtful.

Microaggressions don't have to look like racism or ethnic stereotypes, either. Women of all ethnicities and backgrounds suffer from microaggressions intensely, perhaps more so than many ethnic groups. Consider the last time you heard the term *office mom* used to describe a colleague of yours—most likely a woman—who handles things like office supplies, booking meeting rooms, sifting through others' calendars to find a time to meet, or overall doing the emotional labor of keeping the team happy and working well together. Now consider how often you hear the term *office dad,* if you've ever heard it at all. Sure, we could explain away this difference by pointing out that more women than men work in administrative positions where they would have to handle those sorts of duties, but even this observation hints at a deeper issue: Why is that, exactly? Why do we ask our female colleagues to grab us coffee while they're up, and not our male colleagues? In Japan, it's still entirely common for women in the workplace to brew and bring their male colleagues tea, even if those colleagues are their peers, not their superiors. Additional cultural reasons are at play there (none of them are appropriate explanations, of course, but they exist), but the bottom line remains the same.

Before you assume that microaggressions are only things that minorities and women face, know that even men have to deal with these challenges as well. Consider how often we attach physical strength to masculinity in our society, and then think back to the last time you or a man you worked with was tasked with some form of physical labor that had nothing to do with the job, entirely because you or he was "a strapping young man," or just because you or he was one of the few men available to do the work. This too is a microaggression, assuming that because the male is male, he must be strong enough to do the work or at least stronger than the women he works with. Even if he volunteered, he probably did so because he felt either pressured or expected to, or because his own social programming implies that to not pick up the physical labor would be a blow to his perceived masculinity on the team, an unacceptable cost.

WEIGHING IN ON WHETHER
TO RESPOND TO MICROAGGRESSIONS

Fortunately, the growing research on microaggression offers some ways for marginalized people to respond appropriately without damaging their careers. For example, Kevin Nadal, author, activist, comedian, and professor of psychology at John Jay College of Criminal Justice, focuses on the impact of microaggressions on marginalized people. He developed a complete guide to responding to microaggressions, where he outlines what microaggressions look like on a racial, gender-based, religious, LGBTQ+, or intersectional basis and how a marginalized person can respond appropriately in any of those circumstances.[3] In his paper, Nadal describes a three-step process that people should consider when they first think they've been the victim of a microaggression.

Let's start with an example, torn from my own experiences. Pretend, for a moment, that you come into work to find your laptop unplugged. Your laptop itself hasn't been disturbed, and the charger doesn't seem to have been significantly damaged or moved. It has just been removed from the charging port on your laptop, which is locked at your desk, but now you have to wait for your laptop to charge before you can use it and start your work for the day. Anything could have happened: Someone could have borrowed your charger and then forgotten to plug it in when they returned it. Someone could have jostled your charger, unplugging it and causing your laptop to sit and slowly discharge. Maybe the office cleaning staff accidentally unplugged it when they tidied up around your desk.

Now, pretend it happens again. And again. It happens with enough frequency that you start to question why it's happening and why it seems to only be happening to you. You don't want to bring it up with your colleagues, because it seems like such a small thing and no one else has said anything similar, so you worry it must just be you. You start to think that maybe you should take your laptop and charger home every night or leave a note that says not to unplug your laptop. You start to get a little paranoid, wondering if someone's doing it just to mess with you, specifically. There's no regularity to it, so it's tough to pin down who might be doing it, but all these thoughts distract you from the core issue: Someone is doing something that's making it harder for you to work and causing you anxiety and hassle in the workplace. Is it minor? Absolutely. At most, it only actually costs you a few minutes of work while you wait for your laptop to charge before you can start working. You're not being physically harmed or anything—but it is the kind of prank, accident, or simple slight that has you wondering exactly which of those three it actually is.

Now, when he spoke to Yoon about microaggressions, Nadal suggested asking three questions to determine whether a microaggression has truly occurred:

1. Did this microaggression really occur?
2. Should I respond to this microaggression?
3. And if I do respond, what are my options?

In my laptop-charger example, the answer to number 1 is yes. No one can dispute that what's happening to you is actually happening. As for number 2, well, that depends. Without knowing to whom you should respond, you run the risk of responding to a group of people, like everyone who sits in your vicinity or everyone on your team. A group response could backfire, especially if you're a minority in your workplace and already marginalized. A team-wide email, for example, would come off as passive-aggressive and only further alienate you in the office, especially among people who have nothing to do with what's happening to you and who could easily explain away what you're going through as a simple accident. These responses are normal: Most outsiders, especially when it comes to microaggressions, tend to automatically assume ignorance or accident over intentional malice—which is part of the reason microaggressions are so hard to address. Even if the behavior is an accident, shifting the focus onto the intention of the perpetrator allows the discussion to completely bypass the actual harm of the action.

So let's pretend instead that you can identify the person who's been unplugging your laptop. You don't know why they have been doing it, but you're reasonably sure you know who it is. Maybe they're borrowing your charger on a regular basis, or they have a friend come and sit at your desk and plug their laptop into your charger. Maybe there's an actual explanation. You don't know what it is, but you do know who it is. Since it's causing you to lose productive work time, you now have to ask yourself if you even *should* address the microaggression. You have to consider the person's position, whether they have any seniority over you on the team or whether their leverage with other team members could make your life harder down the line. Will they be willing to stop, regardless of their intent, or will they lie to you and keep doing it? Will you make your work life harder by responding, or is it easier for you to anticipate the microaggression and just endure it? These are the kinds of questions that marginalized people in the workplace have to answer all the time, even before they figure out if they are actually even going to respond: Do I even ask that I not be the one to schedule all the team meetings, or should I just suck it up? Do I go along with my boss making jokes about me busting out "kung-fu moves" on her if she gets on my bad side, or do I tell her not all Asian people know martial arts? Do I tell my colleague that having parents who came from Mexico doesn't mean it's okay to say, "Hola!" every time he sees me?

In some cases, it's easier just to get used to the treatment than it is to wrangle with the complicated defensiveness and other emotions of the person responsible for the microaggression. But even simply absorbing the microaggression has side effects. In a 2017 article for the *Center for Health Journalism*, Gina Torino explains that microaggressions and other toxic behavior in the workplace are tied to poorer health outcomes for people of color.[4] She cites a 2014 survey published in the *American Journal of Public Health* that pointed to day-to-day racist experiences that contribute to chronic-stress disparities across ethnic groups. The survey also found that chronic stress itself is a significant factor in hypertension, another long-term health condition that people of color disproportionately face.[5] Yoon, in her piece in the *Times*, also cites a study in the journal *Suicide and Life Threatening Behavior* that says in no uncertain terms that racial microaggressions contribute to depression and suicidal ideation among people of color.[6]

DECIDING WHEN AND HOW TO RESPOND

So on the one hand, suffering with microaggressions causes real harm, especially in the long term, to the people who choose not to risk their careers or already-tenuous workplace connections by discussing them or calling out offending behavior. But on the other hand, people who do respond run the risk of finding themselves even more marginalized from their colleagues than they were in the first place.

But if you do respond, Nadal's research offers us some suggestions:

1. Ask yourself, if you respond, will your physical safety be in danger? Some people don't take kindly to being called out on any behavior, regardless of how abusive it might be.

2. Even if the person isn't a physical threat, perhaps the individual is a professional or social one—would bringing up the behavior cause problems with this person down the road, either in a professional or social setting?

3. If you don't respond, will that signal that you somehow tacitly approve of that behavior or think it's appropriate? Will you regret it later if you don't?

People of color who have had to cope with racist microaggressions like the ones just mentioned, or queer and transgender people who have had to deal with remarks like "Wow, are they a man or a woman?" or who stifled their reaction when people said, "That's so gay" when describing something they didn't like—all these people already know these questions, even if they haven't voiced them specifically. In fact, most marginalized people run through some version of these questions every time they're confronted with a microaggression and trying to figure out how to respond to it.

But the professional or social consequences of calling out a microaggression are what usually weigh heaviest on our minds. If I confronted the colleague I suspected of unplugging my laptop and told the person to stop, would they just deny it and keep doing it, happy now knowing that they'd gotten under my skin? If I say something to correct the boss who just assumes I'm good at basket-ball because I'm Black, will this person consider me overly sensitive or, worse, aggressive, and will that opinion come up in a future per-formance review?

These questions have no easy answers. After all, the answers often depend on the people you work with and the work environ-ment you're in. In some jobs, I have felt comfortable telling my boss, "Hey, just because I'm Black doesn't mean I can play basketball" (and I really, really can't). But at the same time, I avoided confronting the colleague I thought was unplugging my laptop, because I didn't have proof it was him and, even if I could have proved it was him, I had no proof that he was doing it maliciously. (He could have been charging his laptop with my cable and then just being careless about plugging it back in, which is its own kind of malice, but I digress.)

THE IMPORTANCE OF PSYCHOLOGICAL SAFETY

If you have what we call *psychological safety* in your job, you're more likely to advocate for yourself with the people you work with. If you don't, you won't. Now think about your own job for a moment. If these stories were your story, would you feel comfortable speaking up to your current boss or to a colleague who said something that rubbed you the wrong way? Maybe you'd be comfortable speaking up to one of your colleagues, but not another. There's your answer.

But maybe you've had enough, or you just want to set the record straight for future interactions, or you just want to make it clear that you're uncomfortable with the kind of treatment you've received. If you come on too strong, the person you're speaking with will get defensive and take nothing from the response. Worse, they may assume that *you* are attacking *them* and that they're actually the victim in the situation. This belief will only entrench them further and make it harder for you to make your point and to feel safe in future conversations with them. If all of this sounds unfair—that is, you have to deal with the pain of the microaggression *and* you have to deal with being the one to correct it—you're right. It's not fair. But standing up for yourself is often necessary, and if you feel safe enough to do it, you absolutely should.

THE POWER OF "WHAT DO YOU MEAN BY THAT?"

One technique that has worked for me in moments of microaggression is to ask someone, completely seriously, "What do you mean by that?" Forcing another person to halt the flow of the conversation and reflect on exactly why you asked them what they meant—and forcing them to examine the meaning behind their words—is often enough to signal that they said something wrong. The question signals that they should probably stop short and think again before making a comment like that around you.

I've particularly found this technique helpful when talking with people who will make comments about a group I'm not a member of, or at least not visibly so. If someone makes an anti-Semitic comment, for example, a little stone-faced "What do you mean by that?" or "How did you come to think that?" goes a long way. In most cases, the reaction is embarrassment rather than defensiveness, and that's enough. It's not truly *corrective*, in that I don't dispel the notions that caused the person to believe what they're saying. But it's certainly enough to make them aware that I don't share their sentiment and I'm not the kind of person they should say such things to.

If you prefer an approach that focuses a bit more on educating the person or trying to correct their behavior for the long term, consider, first, letting them know that you're sure their intentions weren't malicious. This approach gives them the benefit of the doubt (although, frankly, some people don't deserve it) and will help stave off the defensiveness. Then you let them know that what they said is harmful and explain why. Ruchika Tulshyan also has a suggestion. "In terms of making people aware," she says, "I like to name behaviors and actions rather than label people. So I have found moderate success with saying 'When you don't invite me to meetings, I feel excluded. Could it be because I'm the only person of color?' rather than, 'You're a racist for not inviting me to these meetings.'" I can vouch for this idea—unfortunately many people, especially privileged ones, perceive the possibility of being labeled racist, sexist, or otherwise discriminatory as somehow worse than the actual harmful treatment they inflict on others. Tulshyan continues, "Some research shows people with privilege can be so immunized by it, they may not even know they're being biased. But if you're met with anything else than genuine desire to learn and improve from the other person, I wouldn't push the issue. It's not the marginalized person's problem to fix!"

SEPARATE THE INTENT OF ACTION
FROM THE IMPACT OF THE ACTION

In 2008, activist, educator, and hip-hop radio veteran Jay Smooth produced a YouTube video where he explained how to tell someone that they sound racist.[7] The entire video is well worth a watch, but the key point is this: We need to separate the *intent* of someone's action from the *impact* of that action. So telling someone that they said something that was racist, sexist, homophobic, transphobic, or otherwise harmful does not—and should not—mean that you're telling them that they are racist, sexist, homophobic, or transphobic or that they hold those beliefs. Unfortunately, in discussions around microaggressions, the perpetrator is quick to conclude that you're saying they're a bad person, not that they did a bad thing. And separating the person's impact from their intentions is key to getting through that fog. After all, even people who are ostensibly actually racist don't want to be called out as such, because our society has largely decided that being racist is a bad thing. So, as we see on social media and in public circles with celebrities and politicians, they'll bend over backward to avoid the label, instead doubling down on their comments or even blaming "cancel culture" or the existence of social media for the repercussions of their own actions.

So to bring it back to microaggressions, when you tell someone that what they said was hurtful or problematic, you'll want to let them know that the action is the issue here, not them as a person. Trust me, I know it sounds like you may be treating the person with kid gloves, and honestly, you probably are, but it helps. This approach is beneficial in another way: It points out that regardless of someone's intentions, their actions can be harmful. The first thing out of your colleague, manager, or even work friend's mouth may be, "Oh! I didn't mean to come off that way," which is an attempt to absolve themselves of the responsibility of their actions by shifting the focus back on their intentions. Because they didn't *intend* to offend, then it couldn't possibly be offensive, right? All should be forgiven!

But that's not the way humans interact. Intentions don't invalidate actions. If you've ever been in a car accident, it's unlikely that you or the person with whom you collided got in the car that morning intending to hit another vehicle, but the damage is still done. You may not intend to get someone else sick when you head to work with the sniffles, but it's possible—even likely—that you will. When you spill a drink on the floor, you didn't intend to give yourself the job of cleaning it up, but, well, you got it anyway. Your actions may not belie your intentions, but good intentions don't pay to repair your vehicle, give you back the sick days you and your colleague will spend recovering, or clean up the spilled drink. After all, that's why we say that the road to hell is paved with good intentions.

Acknowledge the intentions of the person you're dealing with but make it clear that the action still persists. Let them know that you're oh so sure they didn't mean to be hurtful but that it still hurts to hear the kinds of things they said or to have to deal with the kinds of things they did. Let them know you hope they won't do it or say it again. As long as you can let them know that you're not attacking them and that you just want to avoid the situation in the future, the entire conversation should go over smoothly. Or at least as smoothly as possible.

Keep in mind that even if you do everything right, the situation could still go sour. Go in at the beginning knowing exactly how much emotional energy you plan to put into this interaction. At the end of the day, it's not the responsibility of someone who's already marginalized to educate others about what's acceptable and what's offensive, especially on top of the job you're already at work to do. At worst, have a plan to disengage from the conversation if it goes sour. Use something like "Well, I just wanted to clear the air; I hope it doesn't come up again," and move on. At best, you've set your boundaries and clarified that the kind of behavior you're speaking up about isn't acceptable, and that's all you really need to do.

FIND A PLACE TO BE HEARD

Finally, dealing with microaggressions is draining. Whether you call out the behavior or decide it's just not worth it and you try to work around it, dismiss it, or ignore it, the microaggression itself still takes a toll on you. Recognize this, and make sure to take care of yourself. Let yourself feel what you're feeling, whether that's anger, frustration, or sadness. Acknowledge the harm that the event caused you, and give yourself the space and time to recover. I can't stress enough the importance of having someone, especially someone who is part of your community, to talk to about the microaggression. Whether it's a therapist (if you have access to one), mental health services, a company resource group for other employees like you, or even a professional or trade group, it helps to have a group of people who also understand what you're going through to talk to and support you.

However, even informal groups like a company Slack channel or a group chat for you and colleagues you trust can go a long way to making you feel less isolated, alone, and marginalized, especially if you actually are on your own when it comes to your team or your organization. As you'll hear throughout the book, sometimes the best thing for you and your career is to be part of a community that will support you, one that transcends jobs, companies, or even careers. In some of my darkest moments, when I could barely get out of bed to even work from home, much less face the prospect of going into an office filled with faces that looked down at me at worst and ignored me at best, it was a community of fellow journalists of color that saved me. They reminded me that I wasn't alone and that it didn't have to be this way. These understanding friends offered me the help and support that let me know that everything I was going through wasn't just in my head—it was all actually happening, and I didn't have to put up with it. Regardless of why you're marginalized at work, my greatest advice is this: Find a similar community that supports you.

Trust Your Experience

(GASLIGHTING)

As I discussed earlier, someone in my office was sporadically unplugging my laptop from its charger, and yes, it was annoying, and yes, I still think it was a microaggression. When I debated with myself about confronting the person who I thought was unplugging my laptop, I concluded that one of two things was likely to happen: Either he would own up to it but come up with a lie that would explain his behavior ("Oh, I was just charging my laptop/phone/device and forgot to plug it back in!"), or he would undermine the effect of his actions by telling me that he didn't mean it and that I shouldn't take it so seriously. If I explained that because he did it repeatedly, I was sometimes forced to wait to even start my workday while my laptop, having been unplugged for a whole weekend or several days, charged up enough to power on, he might dismiss my complaint. Or if I told him that the unplugging was disruptive enough that I couldn't grab my laptop and go to a meeting at the beginning of my workday, he might also downplay it, saying it didn't happen as often as I made it out to happen and that the impact couldn't have been that significant.

These kinds of dismissals are called *gaslighting*.

Gaslighting occurs when people recharacterize events and actions afterward to cast doubt on the meaning or severity of the actions to the person who was affected by them. It's a way for people who commit acts of abuse to rewrite history to make their actions less malicious or less intentional than they were. Ultimately, gaslighting pushes the responsibility for someone's actions onto the person being wronged, forcing them to reconsider whether they experienced the event the way they thought they did or whether their feelings about what happened to them are even valid.

It's manipulative and often used by malicious actors as a way to force the people they discriminate against or actively marginalize into thinking that they, the marginalized ones, are the ones at fault and didn't consider the intentions behind the actions they've called out. Gaslighting forces the victim to suffer twice over: once from the action and again when the person tries to relive and decipher the meaning behind what happened to them.

Meanwhile, the perpetrator—or in systemic cases, the perpetrator and the people around this person, whether they're friends, allies, or even managers—continues without having to address the bad behavior they've been presented with. "Intention should never supersede impact," Tulshyan told me. "Prioritizing (and forgiving) intention protects perpetrators and the dominant group. We must look at impact. I think the problem is [that] gaslighters turn it into a defense mechanism to absolve themselves of guilt."

YOUR INNER VOICE SPEAKS THE TRUTH

In gaslighting situations, it's important to trust your experiences and your expertise and to document what has happened to you, for future reference. Doing so gives you a way to establish a pattern if you need to. But identifying people who gaslight is the first and most important step, and that's not always easy. Nor is it easy to let go of our own innate desire to get over things and get on with our work, especially if we have to work closely with the people who have wronged us. A person who turns to gaslighting is often relying on you to just look the other way or decide that what they're doing isn't significant enough for you to bring it up openly, so they can continue their behavior. It's petty, for sure, but gaslighting is just another way manipulative or toxic coworkers can marginalize their peers to keep them quiet, on the sidelines. Meanwhile, the perpetrators pick up the glamorous work that will boost their careers, and they get away with being the kind of colleague that wouldn't be tolerated in a more open and transparent work environment.

Combine that with the fact that for people of color, women, and others who are already discriminated against in the workplace, even speaking up about poor treatment by a peer can cost them, careerwise. Consider, for example, a Black woman who is on a team of mostly white colleagues and who may already be saddled with the office housework. If she tries to gently point out that her skills and previous work experience mean she should be leading projects instead of taking notes in meetings, she runs the risk of being permanently labeled as an "angry Black woman." She risks getting the same label if she speaks up about the coworker who keeps telling her clients to work with them instead of her, just to, you know, "reduce confusion and cross-communication." That scenario, although I'm not a Black woman, actually happened to me. A colleague told a personal friend—an excellent writer I'd worked with several times in the past—to stop working with me and to work exclusively with him instead if my friend wanted more and better opportunities at our workplace because he could promote them and I couldn't. But mostly, the colleague said, it was just to "minimize confusion."

Now, had I brought up this colleague's action to my manager, she would have shaken her head and acknowledged that it was bad form and definitely unfortunate, but she would have left it up to me to handle. I was aware of the situation now, she might say, and shouldn't I just be comfortable talking to my colleague about that kind of behind-my-back behavior? In a perfect world—on a team where I had the psychological safety to voice my concerns without repercussions and where I was respected enough to be sure of some resolution—I would have brought it up. But I didn't have that sense of safety, and I didn't feel that level of respect, so I did nothing. I fumed in private with my friend and others who would hear me out and understand where I was coming from, instead of ignoring the episode entirely. The last part of this story is important as well: having people you can communicate with and whom you trust outside the situation where you believe you're being gaslighted.

But even a superior's response can be part of the gaslighting process. A manager who tells you to just work it out or that the issue isn't too significant or who would rather dismiss your concerns instead of addressing them with either you, the other person, or, ideally, both of you is contributing to the problem. They're undermining the seriousness of the issue with you and encouraging you to assume that it's less important than you think it is. They're also placing responsibility for what has happened to you back on you.

All this behavior is by design, though. Even if it's not intentional, it's all intended to make your abuse be your own problem, and not theirs. It's designed to make you second-guess yourself and think twice about doing anything about it or standing up for yourself, even in the smallest ways. If this happens to you repeatedly, it's like being in any toxic or abusive environment. It takes a mental and emotional toll and ultimately adds up psychologically. The working world vastly underestimates how harmful a toxic workplace can be, especially for marginalized people, who have no people to share their experiences with. So how do you identify that what's happening to you is actually gaslighting, and what do you do about it? Here are a few suggestions.

IF IT FEELS WRONG, IT PROBABLY IS, NO MATTER WHAT THEY SAY

This gets into trust-your-gut territory, but I'll say this about people who are socially discriminated against or othered in larger society: You're the best judge of whether something that happened to you was meant, even in small part, to cause offense. You're the best judge of whether that person hurriedly pressed the door-close button on the elevator because they didn't want to share space with someone in a wheelchair. You're the best judge of whether that person asked you to grab coffee for the morning huddle because you're the only woman on the team, not because they figured you lived closer to the doughnut shop. You're the best judge of whether, every time you speak up for yourself, your colleague is only pretending that they're physically threatened by you or, as the colleague says, is "just joking." All those behaviors represent stereotypes and biases that people have about others, and these attitudes cannot be washed away with in-house implicit-bias training, no matter how much HR departments and well-meaning white workers think they can be.

In fact, I distinctly remember sitting at a lunch with a group of teammates and hearing them discuss how wonderful the recent implicit-bias training at our organization had been—training that I'd never been invited to or included in. Ironically, the conversation was clearly going on *around* me to make me think that they were all good people whom I could trust because of their participation and positive thoughts about the training. (As any person of color will tell you, praise for implicit-bias training is far more likely to sound alarm bells in your mind than anything else is.)

"I think there is moderately more awareness of racism in the workplace, and when I've brought it up more recently, people have thanked me and apologized," Tulshyan told me when I asked about how people react when they're called out on their gaslighting. "But by and large, there's defensiveness, tears [white women and their tears!] or denial/attack [see DARVO[1]]. It's extremely tough, especially because experiencing microaggressions (and other discriminatory behaviors) does compound over the years and cause serious harm in the long run. It's never a matter of having a thicker skin. It really does eat away at you, and it's hard to perform at your best when you're being gaslit, excluded, and attacked."

When I asked her how the people who have been gaslighted or who are otherwise marginalized respond when they finally have an advocate, she explained: "Marginalized folks have, by and large, been so relieved when I confirm that what they thought might be incidents of bias . . . are bias," she said. "So often, our coping mechanism is to try and brush it off, to keep the peace at all costs. It can be tremendously validating to look someone in the eye and say, 'No.

That was biased, and you're right to be upset.' Our society still prioritizes the comfort of perpetrators. Never miss the opportunity to validate these feelings."

So trust your instincts. If someone says or does something that crosses the line for you, don't let them or anyone else talk you out of your perception of it. Entertain criticism from trusted sources, of course—if someone you know and trust asks you questions about the event to try to uncover the meaning behind it, that's one thing. But if you speak up for yourself or talk to someone who has some influence over the situation and that person tries to get you to walk back the impact of the event, don't let them. Or if you have to accept their take, understand that it's probably driven more by their own desire to minimize the importance of what happened than by anything else.

FIND PEOPLE OR COMMUNITY YOU CAN TRUST

Speaking of bouncing what happened to you off someone else, it's important to find other people you can talk to explicitly about what's going on and how you've been feeling. Not only does sharing with a sympathetic person make you feel less alone, but it also gives you some friendly faces or voices to share your experiences with that don't have a relationship to the people responsible for gaslighting you. Those people can take a number of shapes: Perhaps it's a counselor or therapist who's helping you work through the issues you face in a toxic environment and who can help you handle the mental health struggles that come along with it. Maybe it's a colleague on a different team—someone who has some perspective on the company culture but doesn't have to deal with your manager or your team.

And if you're part of a marginalized group, consider checking with your company's HR department to see if there's an employee resource group (ERG) for your identity. Not every company where I've worked has ERGs, and some are more prevalent and influential in the corporate culture than others, but if you can find an ERG, it can provide useful insider help. You must, however, be absolutely sure that anything you share is in confidence and not likely to make it back to the people involved in a way you didn't intend. For example, during my tenure at the *Times,* the Black@NYT group was wonderful. I could go to the events the members hosted, hang out on panels they put together, and in general just attend meetings and events without feeling as if I were the only person of color in the world or in a space where people didn't really want me. However, before I worked in journalism, the companies I worked at didn't have groups like that, and if they did, they were generally on a department-by-department basis.

"Racial gaslighting, unfortunately, is so rampant and we are just barely scratching the surface of how prevalent this issue is," Tulshyan said. "I actually think we always know in our gut that something is wrong and what holds us back from confronting our feelings is that recognition that the establishment will most likely not want to support us and rock the boat. This is where that backup could be helpful—check in with people you trust; share information of what happened. Enlist their backup if you bring it up to the organization. But most of all, I found support when I began writing down the incidents—seeing it on paper (or screen) really helped me step back and realize that this was a larger pattern of bias. I can't stress that approach to collecting information on it enough."

Alternatively, you can look for a community outside of a specific job or company. I'd argue that an outside group is a better approach anyway and one you should consider even if you do find a group inside your company that you can rely on. That way, your community can transcend any specific situation you may find yourself in, whether it's a bad team, a bad boss, a bad company, or even a bad career.

STAND UP FOR YOURSELF, THE RIGHT WAY

The final key to doing something about gaslighting is knowing that you don't have to deal with it. Much like microaggressions, gaslighting works because the people who frequently use it do so as a method of abuse and control that's both deniable and quiet. So much so that by design, gaslighting forces you to spend time and energy thinking about the abuse you received and how it would be best to respond in a way that doesn't harm you more than it helps. That mental wrangling, on top of trying to figure out the best avenue to address the situation, if you address it at all, is part of the sting—like an aftershock to the main earthquake, as it were. But here's the thing: You don't have to put up with it. It's really just a matter of going in with your own expectations and boundaries and being prepared to defend those boundaries, no matter what.

This stance is super difficult for early-career employees and for people in precarious positions (and those in precarious positions because of their identity). But it's always good to walk into work on a given day knowing what, exactly, you're willing to put up with and what you absolutely won't. "Too many people think confronting bi-ased behaviors would mean they have to first accept they're a bad person, when to solve this issue it's less about whether you're 'good' or 'bad' and more about how you can prevent this behavior from reoccurring," Tulshyan explained. "I have found some moderate success in saying, 'I believe this wasn't your intent, but this is how it impacted me. Could you please refrain from . . . ?'"

On top of that, it's worth making it clear to your manager what you're willing to accept and where your boundaries are. Sit the person down and say, "Look, I've been seeing this behavior lately from others in the office, and I don't know where it's coming from, but I want to be on the same page with you about how I respond if it happens again." You may have to deal with the stereotypical ele-ments of gaslighting again, of course. Your manager might ask if it's really that important or if the behavior or incident really meant what you think it meant. But it's just as important for you to stop and say, "I know we might disagree on this, but I know what I'm feeling, and unless this is a thing I need to talk to HR about, I just want you to understand that I need to be comfortable speaking up for myself."

Those can be difficult things to say, especially if the manager does say you should probably talk to HR. But even if you do talk to HR, at least you can make the staff aware of what's happening and can stick to your guns. If you don't feel comfortable naming names, focus on the behavior you're experiencing and not the people doing it. That way, you can make it clear to everyone involved that you're taking issue with the way you're being treated, not with the people treating you this way (even if you might, and you probably do). So take some time to think about your personal and professional boundaries. Remember, there's more to life than work, and while there are certainly times when you need to swallow your pride to get through the day at work, you should never swallow your pride in the face of actual mistreatment.

FOCUS ENTIRELY ON ACTION
AND THE IMPACT THE ACTION HAS

The next thing to remember is that when you do stand up for yourself, focus entirely on the action and the impact the action has. Gaslighting 101 is to try to get you to focus instead on the intention of the perpetrator, but watch out for that tactic and refocus the conversation or interaction accordingly. Things like "I know you didn't *intend* this, but *what happened* was . . . , and here's the result." Keeping your focus on the events that occurred over the feelings of the person responsible will ideally keep the conversation on the right track.

Only Spend Time on Work That Gets You Attention

(BEING SEEN)

I n Black households like the one I grew up in, it's not uncommon for parents to tell their children that they have to be "twice as good" as other children not just to succeed, but also to be judged the same way that other children are. It's a very subtle way of introducing Black children to the fact that systemic racism exists, that it rears its ugly head in odd places, and that they'll be the victims of it sooner, not later. Serena Williams has mentioned it, and Michelle Obama gave an entire speech about it in 2015. In her speech, she said the quiet part loud: that you have to be twice as good to get *half as far* as others—with the others ostensibly being white, privileged peers.

As is the case with most Black children, my first experience with systemic racism came in school. Bottom line: To be considered as competent as my white peers, I had to work twice as hard. I had to work twice as hard to be taken seriously or even to be considered a candidate for the same kind of success that my other classmates had taken for granted.

When I decided to pursue physics and astronomy in college, my high school Advanced Placement (AP) physics teacher told me that I'd never finish college. He told me I'd fail the physics AP exams. Spoiler: I passed the AP exams with scores high enough to translate to college credit. I finished both undergraduate programs, and I'm proud of my degrees in both physics and astronomy. I'm also proud of the determination and stubbornness that got me there. I was the only Black student in my physics cohort. I was the only Black student in my astronomy cohort. I quickly became accustomed to doing, behind the scenes, twice the work that a number of my classmates were doing and showing up to office hours more often than my peers did, just to prove my interest and dedication to my studies.

You may find yourself having to work twice as hard because you're a woman working on a team of all men and want them to take you seriously. Or maybe you're the youngest on the team and you feel as if you have to be twice as dependable to prove yourself. Or you might be the oldest on the team and a new hire, and you think you have to work twice as hard to keep up or prove yourself to your younger colleagues. In each of these cases, it might feel natural to bust your ass, but you shouldn't have to. In a just world, we would all be judged on our own merits, especially in the workplace.

But we don't live in a just world. We live in a world where we walk into every space we inhabit carrying a world of social baggage tied to our identities and how other people perceive us, and we have nothing to do with that perception. Even working twice as hard may not make your younger colleagues perceive you as anything but slow and old. Busting your ass won't change the mind of a manager who's convinced that they shouldn't promote you, because you'll just get married or pregnant and then quit. Staying after hours every night may show your team you're committed, but it won't change the mind of your colleague who's convinced that Black people are lazy.

But what's the alternative? After all, a wealth of research suggests that marginalized employees—and specifically employees of color—actually do have to be twice as good as their white or male counterparts to be seen as equal in the eyes of often white managers and executives. Those same managers and executives often perceive their judgment as objective and without bias. In a 2015 paper published for the National Bureau of Economic Research, Costas Cavounidis and Kevin Lang, both of Boston University, indicated that minority employees, specifically Black American employees, are often scrutinized more heavily on the job than their white counterparts. Companies spend more resources monitoring their Black employees than they do for their white employees and consequently tend to overdiscipline the Black staff for minor infractions and offer less praise than they offer the white staff. And because Black employees are so often overdisciplined, they wind up with worse performance reviews, fewer raises and opportunities for promotion, and a stunted career path. They're also more likely to be laid off or fired, and when they are, they spend more time unemployed, which makes future employers similarly wary and likely to overscrutinize their work in the future, setting off the whole cycle anew. Meanwhile, white employees get the benefit of the doubt, and while their Black colleagues would be let go for the same infractions, white employees are often given a second chance.

Gillian White, writing about the study in the *Atlantic,* got to the heart of the "twice as good" argument: "In order to keep a job, black workers also must meet a higher bar. Only in instances where black workers are monitored and displayed a significantly higher skill level than their white counterparts would they stand a significant chance of keeping their jobs for a while, the researchers found. But even in instances where the productivity of black workers far exceeded their white counterparts, there was still evidence that discrimination persisted, which could lead to lower wages or slower promotions."[1]

So on one level, making sure that you're seen—and that your work is appreciated and noticed by your colleagues and especially by your managers—can go a long way toward eliminating how marginalized you may be at work. After all, part of the cycle of being marginalized is that you and your work are dismissed or put off to the side, even when it's incredible work. Even if you do great work, you find that it just doesn't get the attention other people's work gets, or your colleagues don't give you the same credit and accolades that other people get for their work, even when it's less impressive on its face. When I spoke to Katherine Crowley and Kathi Elster, authors of a number of excellent books, including *Working with You Is Killing Me*, about management (more on that later), they agreed that so often, being marginalized comes down to not being seen, even if you're making efforts to be present or involved. Making sure you get some face time with the people who matter—namely, your manager and other people in power—is incredibly important to changing the perception that you're doing no work of value or no work at all. Essentially, even when you're not working on your job, you're working on making sure your work is being seen. Again, you have to work twice as hard and be twice as good.

In the *Atlantic* piece, White pointed out that while this work-twice-as-hard approach does work, it's more like treading water instead of doing something to obtain actual parity with your privileged peers.

Her observations track with my experience, too. Sure, being twice as good can keep you gainfully employed, give you decent performance reviews, and get you recognition as someone who's doing their job, but it doesn't avail you consideration for promotions, awards, or the spotlight-heavy work that we'll discuss later. In short, being twice as good may keep you where you are, but it doesn't place you anywhere beyond that. Then, the other edge of the sword starts to cut as well. You feel burned out, fatigued, and unappreciated. You start to dread going to work, knowing you're giving your job your all and then some, only to see more mediocre colleagues promoted or praised, while you're left tired, dejected, and wondering whether you should just be happy to have a job in the first place.

Of course, in an ideal world, no one would have to be running at 100-plus percent all the time. Just as your privileged colleagues have the freedom to be mediocre from time to time, you should have the luxury of sometimes doing just enough to finish a task and not have to wrap it up in pretty paper and a bow. We could all be judged on the merits and qualifications we bring to the table.

BE JUDICIOUS WITH YOUR TIME

Unfortunately, we don't live in that ideal world, and the key is instead to be smarter than the people you have to deal with, as opposed to just working harder than they do. So how do you just work smarter than everyone else? You start by paying attention not just to what you have to do at work but also to why you're doing it. What are your priorities? What are your team's priorities or your boss's priorities? And then, step back and ask yourself, "How does the work that I'm doing fit into those priorities?"

It may sound a little underhanded here, because you're trying to game the system of work entirely, but ultimately you want to make sure that you don't spend your valuable time on anything except the work that gets you the most attention and earns you the most praise. Everything else floats to the sidelines. It's easier said than done, of course, but part of being twice as good is knowing what people consider *good work* and what they consider *everyday work*. We'll dive a bit deeper into those distinctions later, but think about it like this: You can succeed by doing an appropriate amount of work as long as you're smart about what work you choose to do, when you do it, and how you communicate the work that you're doing. If you excel at the important things and then get the smaller things done on your own time (or even if some of those smaller things slip through the cracks entirely), you'll be recognized for that great work. Even better, if you can come to instinctively understand which aspects of the work have a higher impact than the rest, you'll be in a better position to first tackle the things that will matter the most to your career, and you'll know where to put your energy.

DON'T WORK TWICE AS HARD; JUST BE TWICE AS SMART

To work twice as smart, you start by learning how to prioritize the work you have to do according to not just your own career goals but also the goals of your team or manager. Making these people your allies, if you can, is the first step to making sure your work is respected and you're not critically overworked. So while you may think that doing your work in the order it was received is the best approach, it's only effective if your manager is waiting for you to handle the things they gave you first and if nothing they gave you later down the line is more important. As a project manager, I used to call the important tasks—those that have to be done before anything else can get done—the *critical path*. The critical-path tasks are the ones that hold everyone else up and that everyone later remembers as the big stepping-stones to successfully finishing a project.

Now if your manager is anything like the managers I've had, they'll turn to you and say, "Everything is a priority," or "It's all important," and then just walk away. Don't get mad about that uninformative response, as much as it really is a cop-out. It means one of two things or possibly both: First, the manager doesn't have the time or mental space to try to organize your tasks. That's on them, frankly. They should help you prioritize, but not every manager is forthcoming. If you're a manager and someone on your team asks you to help them organize their work by priority, *please* help them do it. It'll benefit you, too. Or, second, the manager really does consider everything to be of some level of importance and wants to see how you organize it yourself. I've worked with managers like the latter. For these people, picking what was most important and most time-sensitive to work on was part of my job, and I was judged on how well I could juggle multiple tasks. So, unfortunately, the onus is on you now to figure out what to do.

First, observe your manager. Even if they don't want to tell you which clients or projects are the most important or which tasks you should dive into first and which can wait, pay attention to your manager's clues. Consider what they discuss in meetings, who they talk about the most when they're assigning you work, and which projects they seem to give you the most work for.

Not every task is equal, as you probably already know. If your manager only ever discusses project A in your team meetings or one-on-ones, but you've been working on project C, it's probably a safe bet that project A is really the one that's stressing your manager out or, at the very least, is at the top of their mind. Consider shifting your time over to match the things your manager is spending their time on—or at least the one they're most worried about. That way, you're aligning your priorities with your boss's priorities, and that's always a sure bet when you're trying to work smarter. After all, if your boss is anxious about project A but you keep talking about project C, something they ostensibly know is important but aren't concerned with, they'll just think you're spinning your wheels or doing busywork. If you agree with them on the importance of project A and let them know you're hard at work on it, they're more likely to look at you as someone who's capable of taking a burden off their shoulders and filling in for them when necessary. This approach is key to making sure your manager considers you for important projects.

Second, use your own professional network or at least the office grapevine. If you can trust them, your colleagues surely know all about the projects and unfinished work your team is facing. If you have good relationships with other departments, ask on your own behalf about timelines and deadlines. That will help you avoid asking your manager for that kind of clarity and will help you connect with other people at your company. Do this with caution, obviously. Not every manager takes kindly to employees talking around them. But if you frame it up as though you're trying to save your manager time and get your work done more efficiently, your effort will go over better. Plus, it will give you valuable intel from your coworkers about how well certain projects are going and how important or influential the projects are to the organization as a whole.

When I was a project manager, before I even got into journalism, I quickly learned not to bother my direct manager for every update or question about the importance of a given project. By getting answers from other sources, I became a clearinghouse of information and someone the boss would rely on for project updates. It was a good place to be, but it required maintaining many connections and open communication channels with other people at the company, and that can be its own job sometimes.

BE AVAILABLE

It helps to be organized, but it's even better to make it clear to everyone involved that they can reach out to you anytime. This level of involvement may feel like another job on top of your job, but this is where the "twice as talented" comes in. Marginalized employees simply don't have the benefit of being mediocre the way their privileged colleagues might—we have to be out there setting up coffee chats, booking meetings when it's important, and picking up the phone when we're concerned about something instead of sending an email and hoping they get back to us. It sucks, but again, people of color and queer employees are probably already used to being judged differently for the work they do.

In short, if both my white male colleague and I promise our boss to have an update on the boss's desk by the end of the day, and both of us send emails to our respective contacts asking for said update early in the day but neither of us gets a response, we face different consequences. My colleague is likely to go home at the end of the day comfortable in the knowledge that if the boss comes asking for that update tomorrow, he can say, "I reached out to my contact for an update, but they never got back to me. I'll have it for you as soon as I get ahold of them." But if I said the same thing, my boss's first reply would be a likely "Well, did you call them? How did you reach out? Call them now." And I'd have to defend why I chose to email in the first place instead of scheduling a meeting or picking up the phone.

YOU HAVE TO TALK TO PEOPLE

You'll be held to a different standard, so if you hold yourself to a different standard from the get-go, you won't just succeed, you'll thrive. Talk to people, and don't be shy. You don't have to be an extrovert to do this, either. I'm certainly not. Make your conversations as informal as possible, and give people the opportunity to come to you instead of forcing yourself to go to them. Ask if you can swing by their desk to chat. Don't make a formal appointment. Just do it sometime when you feel the need to get up and stretch. If you, like me, feel more comfortable with a hot drink in your hands, propose you two grab coffee and catch up on the project. Not only will you get the information you need to be successful at your actual job, but you'll also meet and engage with people who can appreciate your work and talents, even if they don't hear about those talents through your manager.

I know that reaching out sounds difficult, especially if you—like me—have anxiety when it comes to putting yourself out there with other people. There's a time and place for texting and Slacking and instant messaging your colleagues. Virtual chatting is easier than strolling by their desk, but I heartily suggest doing it, especially if you feel up to it. You can use something like refilling your water bottle as an excuse to see them and say hello for a few moments. But beyond looking for excuses to do it, there's something more powerful and more personal to actually asking a colleague to grab coffee with you one afternoon or suggesting that you two grab a drink (or an ice cream or something, if you prefer not to drink) after work to talk about the project you're working on. It goes a long way to cutting through a lot of the office politics and helping you connect with your colleagues on a one-on-one basis.

If you're really anxious about connecting with a colleague in person, set an end time for yourself. You can then tell your colleague you just want to grab a drink but you have to be home before a given time. This way, you have a hard stop and you'll know that any potential awkwardness will be over. But trust me, putting in that hour or so of social anxiety will pay dividends back at the office. Plus, you never know, you may actually make a real personal friend, not just a professional connection.

WORK BACKWARD

Here's an old-school productivity tip that usually works for everyone, regardless of their identity: Work backward. If you know roughly when the projects you're working on will come to a head, work backward from that date to figure out what you have to do to meet that deadline. This practice works even if—and perhaps especially if—the project's success has nothing to do with you specifically. A great way to make allies in any job, regardless of who you are, is to take an active interest in the success of your colleagues. I can't tell you how many times I completely changed focus after looking at a project timeline and realizing that if I didn't focus on project B instead of project K, project B simply wouldn't get done on time. Granted, my job as a project manager was to monitor those timelines, and that's something that a lot of people don't get to see. But asking your colleagues or your boss when something is going to go live or when they want to see the project finished entirely will help inform which things you should work on first, even if your manager isn't too keen on telling you what's most important to them.

ORGANIZE YOUR THOUGHTS, NOW AND FOREVER

Finally, once you've settled on your priorities and you know what you want to tackle first, put it in writing. Give yourself a plan of attack for the work you have to do, and organize your to-dos according to what those big, important projects are versus the busywork that's less important (but still has to get done!). Then, whenever you have the opportunity to share that list with your manager, let them know that this is the way you're tackling your work, and ask them to let you know if that works for them. Remember, being seen and having your manager know what you're working on and how you're prioritizing the work you're doing are key ways to make sure you're visible and not marginalized into invisibility. Don't be shy—your privileged colleagues certainly won't be.

It's one thing to ask, "What should I be working on?" and it's another to say, "I'm working on this. Does that work for you?" I've found that more managers—especially those reluctant to engage their employees for whatever reason—are likely to sign off on your plan of attack if you're the one who came up with it. Try to get that agreement in writing too, even if you just send them your plan via email and ask them, "Is this okay with you?" Even a quick reply from them—"Yeah, sure"—is enough to bring up in a performance review later if they complain that you're not working on the important things and instead spinning your wheels. You'll be able to respond that you organized your tasks and shared what you were working on with them, and they agreed that your approach was okay. It may not be enough to change the outcome, but it's certainly better than the old "well, you didn't tell me what to do!" defense, and it's a good way to cover your ass.

HOLD YOURSELF ACCOUNTABLE

In that same vein, use this information to hold yourself accountable. After all, telling other people what you're going to do is one thing, but making sure you actually deliver is another. You want to communicate to everyone that you're capable and talented and that your skills and your presence in the room don't need to be questioned. I've found that one of the best ways to remind people that you have a right to be in the room with them, and deserve to be there, is to follow through on what you say. Don't get me wrong, it sucks that you'll encounter people who don't believe this by default, but as my mother used to say, "Don't give them any more ammunition for the guns they so desperately want to use against you."

So make sure that when you commit to a specific set of priorities, you deliver on them. And if you need to reorganize or change things up for whatever reason, take the extra step of communicating those changes to your manager and any partners involved in other departments or teams.

RADICAL TRANSPARENCY

Sometimes, keeping your work close to the vest is important—and you may still need to do that for some things—but radical transparency also helps show everyone that you're open and productive and have nothing to hide. It shows others that the engine is always running and you're always doing great things. Plus, this approach also helps you keep track of the work you're doing, so if you ever wind up in an elevator with an executive and they say something like "So, what are you working on?" you'll have an answer ready.

Much of the advice in the rest of the book involves making sure that you can manage your work effectively and that you're properly protected and more in touch with your work. Sometimes you'll want to follow this advice when dealing with other people, like in a conversation with your manager about how you're doing in general or during a performance review. Or, at worst, you might follow this advice when you're deciding whether to leave the job entirely. More important, though, you'll follow this advice for yourself—it's a gift to your future you, so to speak. You're not just being twice as smart so that your employer can keep you around; you're being twice as smart on your own behalf. You're making sure that you never feel directionless in your work or feel as if everything is crashing down on you at once (or at least, if it is, you know what those things actually are). You're also becoming keenly aware of the work you do, what you don't have time to do, and whether the work on your team is being assigned fairly.

This point is an important one, and critical for marginalized groups. Often, we don't get work assigned to us fairly, and sometimes, the office favorite wins the speaking gig at the next conference while we're assigned to making sure their PowerPoint deck looks good. Or maybe we're the one who does the research for the annual report, but it's not our name that goes on it. Unfortunately, marginalized workers are often relegated to the kind of work that has to be done but that rarely amounts to their praise or professional growth, while their privileged counterparts see their names in lights or get to work on banner projects, sometimes despite a difference in skill or experience. Let's now look at what we can do about these inequities.

Office Housework Will Never Get You Ahead

(GETTING THE GLAMOUR WORK)

Think about your previous jobs. Have you ever had someone who everyone in your organization looked up to as the "office mom"? Was it you? Maybe that person scheduled the meetings, organized the calendars, ordered lunch for those meetings, took notes or minutes, and sent out agendas before and after those gatherings. Maybe they kept the supply closet stocked, kept pain medication on hand in case a coworker needed it, or knew the best place to get the good coffee. Maybe it was this individual's job to know and do all these things, and the person was an administrative assistant for your team. But maybe—and, sometimes, more likely—they were a team member who just picked up those additional responsibilities on top of the work they were already doing.

Now think about those previous jobs again. Odds are, you never had an "office dad," whose job it was to do all those same things, unless he really was an administrative assistant. Before we go too much further, think about that for a moment. Why is it so often the women on your team who are responsible for making sure guests have access to the Wi-Fi, for taking notes during the team meeting, or for coming in early to bring bagels and coffee? This story may be familiar to some of you, and it has happened to more people than I can count, especially women of color and other women in the workplace.

Ruchika Tulshyan, CEO of Candour, has written extensively about the dichotomy between office housework and glamour work.[1] She explained why you've probably never seen an office dad. It is, she told me, "very much due to prevailing gender expectations of women being helpful and nurturing. It's harmful and unnecessary; we need managers to keep an eye out for office housework and ensure it's being assigned fairly, not along gender and racial lines."

That kind of housework—the note taking, mass emailing, snack getting, calendar managing, and so forth—is all work that keeps the team running smoothly, so someone needs to do it. And it's still seen as women's work.

Joan C. Williams and Marina Multhaup, writing in the *Harvard Business Review* about research from the Center for WorkLife Law at the University of California, are credited for coming up with the term *office housework* to refer to the kind of admin work that "keeps things moving forward, like taking notes or finding a time everyone can meet" and "work that's important but undervalued, like initiating new processes or keeping track of contracts."[2] And, of course, office housework is work that needs to be done but doesn't make the company money. And because it is seldom directly tied to company goals or performance indicators, it's "far less likely to result in a promotion than chairing an innovation or digital transformation committee," say Williams and Multhaup.

Contrast office housework with work that earns people promotions, is noticed by management, and makes the company money.

Williams and Multhaup call that kind of work *glamour work* and describe it in *Harvard Business Review* as work that "gives you the opportunity to stretch your skills with a new challenge and can lead to your next promotion. It's the project for a major client, the opportunity to build out a new team, or the chance to represent the company at an industry conference." In other words, glamour work is work you want to spend your time doing. It's the stuff you want to do, as opposed to the stuff you have to do, and it's the work that truly deserves your time.

I contacted Williams to talk about the concept of office housework versus glamour work, and she explained that it was actually her daughter's idea. "My daughter and I coined the term *office housework* in 2014," she said. "Little did I know that seven years later, male reporters would be calling me and knowing all about it. I was going like, 'Well, that's successful dissemination.'"

GLAMOUR WORK CONTRIBUTES TO REACHING SUPERSTAR STATUS

So in short, office housework may be the things that have to get done, but that work is often in the background, away from the eyes of decision makers. And while it may keep the organization or team working smoothly toward the group's collective goals, office housework is highly unlikely to be the kind of thing brought up at your next performance review. Nor will it earn you accolades from your colleagues (at least, not until you leave the job, and everyone says that they don't know how they'll get by without you).

Glamour work, on the other hand, gets you promoted and earns you fame either on your team or across the company and even potential appreciation across your whole industry as a subject-matter expert. It turns individual contributors into valued "superstar" workers with more job security than others, because managers will actively notice the superstars' absence and will have to fill the hole they leave behind if they exit the company or are poached by a competitor.

Williams and Multhaup's research also indicates that women and workers of color are often assigned the office housework. Unfortunately, scheduling appointments, drafting memos, and taking care of the collective needs of the team always seem to fall to the women team members, including women of color and younger women. Meanwhile, white and male coworkers are often given (or assume for themselves) the glamour work, regardless of whether their qualifications or desires are appropriate. So dissecting who gets what work, why, and how both employees and managers can assign work more fairly is essential to making sure everyone has the opportunity to bring their fullest selves to their jobs.

Tulshyan explained that there's definitely a gender element, but there's another racial element as well. "I have seen white women sometimes progress even when they do office housework, because they're seen as a team player. But I can't recall seeing a woman of color get rewarded through advancement opportunities for it," she said. "My sense is this expectation exists because of prevailing stereotypes by race *and* gender for women of color to be servile, as our historical oppression has dictated us to be.

"Research shows women and people of color are more likely to be assigned these tasks and face pushback when they decline. The simple answer for why women and people of color get assigned it is . . . gender and racial expectations on who is expected to be helpful and as a result, less leader-like."

For example, when I worked at the *Times*, the team I joined was in the middle of a number of exciting new projects. One of them was a newsletter, dedicated to the stories our team worked on and published, and while I knew it had been in the works for a long time before I joined the team, I was hoping I'd be able to help out with it. I knew it would be glamour work—the kind of work that would connect directly with our readers and draw praise across teams at the newspaper. I also knew that as an editor on the team, I'd be working on and publishing stories that I would love to highlight in the newsletter. So when it came time to launch, I asked to participate.

The immediate reaction I got from one of my colleagues was interest and willingness to let me help from time to time, but the underlying message was that I wasn't really wanted. Even as I pressed, repeatedly offering to lend a hand or even fill in when my colleague was on vacation or otherwise out of the office, he declined, preferring instead to spend money on freelance writers—usually friends or people he wanted to work with—to do it instead, leaving me out in the cold. It was irritating, but I realized at that point that I was specifically being excluded from the glamour work that, as I'd predicted, was popular and resonated with other teams and people around the paper. I even brought it up to my manager, who agreed that it was an issue but did nothing to rectify it. My manager probably decided it was easier to tell me that it was an issue I had to solve myself than it would be to step in, say something, and potentially cause tension.

That kind of isolation and marginalization became commonplace at that job. I especially felt limited in getting the glamour work that would showcase my abilities to people who had the power to decide whether my skills would be valued on their teams or elsewhere around the paper. In another instance, I was invited to regular meetings with our team responsible for promoting our work to other media outlets, arranging interviews, and pitching our reporters and editors as subject-matter experts to outlets looking to speak to us about our stories. Slowly, over time, I found myself excluded from those meeting invitations, and as a consequence, the stories that I worked on never appeared in those other publications and never found mention in our oh-so-popular newsletter. Only when a story I worked on turned into a viral sensation (something that happened with enough regularity that I was proud of it regardless) could people not avoid approaching me: "Hey, Alan, can you connect me with the person who wrote that? PR would like to chat with them!"

YOU HAVE THREE JOBS

Ultimately, I just assumed that this was how it was going to be in my position or on the team I was on. Some teams at the *Times* were far more cohesive, more collaborative, more inclusive. Others were more disparate, more decentralized, and more individualistic. I thought I'd wound up on an individualistic team, where it was more or less up to me to make a name for myself around the building. But the problem with this solution is that when you're a person of color and as cheerful and (hopefully!) easygoing as I am, you still have the daunting responsibility of having to do your work, exceeding the standards required of the organization so you can get noticed, and making friends, ingratiating yourself to other editors, managers, directors, and team leads. If I had it to do over again, I would have worked harder to overcome my initial shyness at meeting some of those colleagues and editors. I would have tried to harness the welcoming energy they gave me when I was a new colleague and stood in front of their faces, instead of hoping they would muster it up again later if I came knocking.

Some of those people did continue with their welcoming attitude. Some, like the editor of the business desk at the *Times*, actively sought me out, gave me chances to work with her, and appreciated what I did. Others by and large appreciated my willingness to help but were so busy with their own projects that they didn't even know *how* I could help.

Make those connections when they're fresh, and try to habituate yourself into working with as many people and on as many teams as possible, especially if you're in an environment like my workplace, where it was largely up to you to be self-directed and where there were few consequences to marginalizing someone. Had I early on worried a little less about how I and my work would be received by the people who were actually glad to meet me, and had I spent more time going to lunch with them and sharing ideas, I would probably have been more successful.

You have three jobs, in short: being nice and nonthreatening; being good at what you do (twice as good, to be considered worthy of the space you take up); and being popular and strategic, playing the workplace game of politics and allegiances. And of course, when you have the social baggage of being a member of a marginalized group, you have to work harder than your privileged colleagues at all three.

My colleagues didn't have the social baggage that comes with being a Black man when they decided to be assertive and ask for the things they needed or to stand up and propose a new project that they wanted to lead. They didn't have to worry about being seen as overly aggressive, having their qualifications and their skills in doubt because of who they were or even because of how long they'd been at the paper. They didn't have to see the wry smiles of contempt cross their coworkers' faces when they pitched an idea in a meeting the way I saw those faces. Nor did my coworkers have to meet some unspoken standard for "good" that would never have been openly communicated to me.

FAIR ACCESS IS NOT A GIVEN RIGHT IN THE WORKPLACE

And yet, I persisted. But in my desire to turn the situation around and focus on my work—to be a great editor who commissioned great writers and fresh voices, to hold a steady line on editing and only publish high-quality service journalism, and to be responsible for some of the paper's most popular stories, all of which I did, there can be no doubt of that—I missed something important: I was taking on the housework. I was doing the things that needed to be done for the team to function and be successful, and for managers to look at our team collectively. Instead of saying to themselves, "Wow, Alan's doing great work there," the managers would say, "Wow, that team is knocking it out of the park. I'm glad they're doing so well."

And while I continued being responsible for the housework, other colleagues were happily picking up the glamour work—basing which stories they would edit on who they got to work with and how high-profile the story would be instead of on the story's journalistic merit or reader service it would represent. They picked projects that made sure everyone knew their name, less concerned about what their work did for the team or even for the paper itself. And on one level, I don't blame them for that—it's a smart move that builds a personal brand, one that can transcend any particular job, team, or organization. And frankly, everyone should try to do the same, to an extent. It's the kind of work that turns you into a superstar, someone who management is reluctant to let go because of the impact your departure would have on the team or the company. A manager will often fight to retain these superstars should they express the desire to take their skills elsewhere. Unfortunately, I wasn't able to establish myself in this way.

"That definitely happens to men of color," Williams explained. "It's the single most important finding we have. It's like hundreds of graphs about lots of different industries. If you ask people, 'Do [you] get fair access to career-enhancing assignments?' . . . 87 percent in one sample say, 'Yes, I get fair access,' and they're all white guys." Williams was referring to a study of workplace equity she worked on with architects. She also went on to share some other elements of her research, including the worker-bee mindset: "The effect of the worker bee is someone who doesn't complain and works hard. Keeps their head down and avoids confrontation." So who claims both that they are worker bees and have to be worker bees? "One-third of white men, 55 percent of women of color, 63 percent of Black women," Williams explained. For "men of color in general, it's 41 percent. White women, 48 percent. That's the central logic . . . is that you're expected to be a worker bee, not a go-getter." In short, women, especially women of color but also all people of color, wind up in positions where they're generally expected to keep their heads down and take the work that's assigned to them. Meanwhile, men, specifically white men, have the psychological safety in their careers to work under the assumption that they should bring their A game and try to excel.

But back to the housework versus glamour work. I found that over time, when I did have the opportunity to talk with others about my work, I would refer to our team as a group of "fiercely independent" journalists. I'd explain that my colleague ran the newsletter and I, as I often put it, "did everything else, with the help of our trusty assistant," who also, after years of being overlooked and overworked, eventually left. For more than a year, I focused almost entirely on doing the legwork of keeping our section afloat.

After all, as an editor, my job was to find and connect with writers who had interesting stories to tell, commission them to tell those stories, edit their work, help them develop their reporting and writing skills, and, finally, get their work ready to publish, of course, to the standards of our organization. So I did that. A lot. In fact, for several months, I was the only editor publishing stories with any regularity, working quietly but diligently behind the scenes and promoting those stories as often as I could. But it didn't take long for me to realize that doing the housework (and doing it well, I might add) wasn't the only place I should be spending my time. I noticed that in some cases, the things I worked on didn't enjoy the same exposure as did the things others worked on. My projects were not promoted or publicized. There were levers that our organization could use to make sure our readers saw the work that we did, but those levers didn't get pulled for me the way they got pulled for other people.

STRATEGIC RELATIONSHIPS ARE ONLY ONE PIECE

Now before I go further, I don't think these slights were microaggressions or even based *exclusively* on race or the racial dynamics of the people I worked with. I do, however, think that because of those racial dynamics, because I was an outsider who was new to the organization, someone who didn't have the stereotypical background that would have been palatable to a lot of the people I worked with, *and* because I was focused on the housework (because it was the only work I could pick up, partly because of those racial dynamics), I didn't have the friendships and the connections that would have made other people pull those levers for me. I wasn't chummy with the guy on the social team who would make sure my stories got promoted or the folks who decided whether the stories I worked on were worth including in mobile news alerts or should be sent to syndication partners or other news organizations for consideration. In fact, it wasn't until another employee of color on our team (who subsequently left the team) pulled me aside and told me that I needed to spend more time forging those strategic relationships, making those phone calls, and setting up those lunch and coffee meetings, or I'd get left behind and forgotten. I'd had an inkling of the importance of schmoozing like this before the conversation, but up until that point, I had hoped that excelling at my job would, in itself, force people to notice the work I was doing and would have the same effect as socializing did. Spoiler alert: It didn't. She (and I'm grateful to her for doing this, make no mistake) disabused me of that notion. That was when I understood fully that doing my job was, in fact, only part of my job.

YOU CAN'T JUST PUT YOUR HEAD DOWN AND DO GOOD WORK

A lot of this might sound familiar to anyone who has worked in a high-pressure or even remotely competitive work environment. As much as you might wish that just doing your best work and being good at what you do is enough to get you ahead, sometimes it just isn't enough. And add on top of that being a member of a marginalized group, and you have an even finer line to walk between being good at what you do and being nonthreatening and palatable to the people around you.

This fine line exists because those of us in marginalized groups—regardless of what group that may be—are often socialized to put our heads down and focus on doing good work. We must be twice as good at the task at hand and should not advocate for ourselves, because our self-advocacy is often seen as aggression, disobedience, or insubordination. We don't "know our place" when we speak up and demand what we need to get our jobs done, while our privileged peers are just being "assertive." A white man who stands up to the boss and explains confidently that if his team's budget request isn't approved, the team will fail, and the company doesn't want to see that happen, is lauded as a "go-getter" and "confident" for being passionate about defending his people. A woman who does the same is "bitchy" and a "ball-buster," and her concerns aren't worth taking seriously, because she's "overly emotional" or "sensitive" or, even worse, "hysterical" or "sassy."

So instead we relegate ourselves to the office housework, the things that keep the team cohesive and that keep everything running, because it's the only way we know to make ourselves essential to the organization. And as much as we should be allowed to do that and then to shine when we want to or when our skills let us, those glamour opportunities go to the loudest guy in the room instead. He's the one who stands up, full of confidence but empty of skill, and says, "I can do that," because he knows that the task will get his name in lights.

When I asked Williams about this, she cited more data she has collected, specifically among employees who claim they have equal access to desirable assignments, as in the glamour work that will boost your career. Of the white men she interviewed, 85 percent believe they have equal access to choice assignments. The proportions of other people who believe they have equal access are as follows: 75 percent of men of color, 62 percent of women of color, and specifically 50 percent of Black women. "The difference between white men and Black women architects, 35 percent," she said. But what about Black men architects, specifically? Funny you should ask: "We don't have Black men," she answered. "Of course, you can't ever get data on Black men [architects], because there aren't enough in the field. A colleague of mine said it's the metaphysically perfect situation: where you have so much oppression, you can't even document oppression."

THE ART OF ADVOCATING

Fixing inequitable work assignments requires two approaches. First, managers need to learn to assign work more fairly. They also need to resist the urge to be defensive when someone tells them that they're giving in to the loudest person in the room or that they're playing into their own implicit or subconscious biases. And second, those of us who find ourselves saddled with the office housework also need to stand up and advocate for ourselves and our skills, explain that the work is being assigned unfairly, and ask for the same opportunities that our privileged coworkers receive.

Let's start with the second approach. It's a bit more important than the first because, well, first it's actionable, something you can tackle in your life right away. And while it's not your problem or responsibility to fix structural racism and inequality in your workplace, you do have to look out for yourself.

As much as you may think that you're going to just drop all the housework and not do anything until you get a fair shot at some of the glamour work, that's actually the worst thing you can do. I've watched colleagues and friends wind up getting fired because they came to work one day wanting a fresh start and a fair shake, and they told their manager that they weren't going to do the busywork anymore. Their managers, instead of asking why or recognizing that there was a problem to be addressed, just did what their prejudices (at worst) or their social conditioning (at best) demanded: They dismissed the problem employee for not doing what the employee had been asked to do and for not following through on job responsibilities. I've talked to too many employees of color— usually, women of color—who wound up on the wrong side of a manager, usually a male manager, because they weren't appropriately deferential or respectful to the boss when they complained about being stuck booking meetings and ordering lunch while their colleague of the same (or lesser) skill was tasked instead with gathering reports for management or, worse, presenting those reports to the boss in the same meeting that the woman of color booked and catered.

KEEP GOING AND KEEP TRACK

So instead, keep going. I know this advice sounds awful, but keep going and keep track of how often you do the housework. Also keep track of how often your colleagues are offered glamour work that you have the skills—but not the opportunity—to do well. Do what you do, and do it well, for sure, but then when you see a chance to take the next step or grab hold of one of those glamour opportunities, and you don't get it, pull your manager aside and talk with this person. Say that you'd really like the assignment and that you can't help but notice that you've been regularly overlooked for projects like this. Explain that you've been keeping track of how long and how often you've been stuck doing the housework—being the glue that holds your team together—and you'd really like a chance to put your skills to work and an opportunity to shine. If the manager doesn't think your skills are up to snuff, be ready to defend your capabilities—after all, you most likely know your skills better than anyone else does, and you know the best, most honest way to compare yourself with your peers so that your manager will understand. But also don't hesitate to use cold, hard data to make your case. You know how often, exactly, you've been doing the housework. You know how many potential opportunities you wanted to pick up but were overlooked for. You can probably name them, and you should name them to your boss. Clarify how many things your boss has overlooked you for. Whether it's promotions, transfers, or just specific projects and presentations that should have been yours, let your manager know you're aware of all of them. Your boss can ignore your subjective statements about your own and your peers' qualifications but can't ignore who has been given which assignments.

And of course, if your manager does ignore it, it might be time to take your skills and consider a transfer to another department or another job entirely. More on that later. But for now, keep good track of the kind of work that you and your peers are assigned, and note whether your work is housework or glamour work. If you're lucky, you might find that some of the housework you've been doing can become glamour work if you tweak it just so. For example, you could turn a report that you have to compile and email weekly into an in-depth presentation to your management about the data you collected for that report and why it's important. But if the data is not important, then into the housework pile it goes.

Tulshyan elaborated. "It is rare to see the person who completes office housework promoted," she said, "even though we want to believe that the team player will get promoted. But in many cases, advancement doesn't have that much to do with this." She explained that her go-to advice, both in general and in her piece for the *Harvard Business Review,* is to push back gently with language like "I worry that if I do this, I won't be able to excel at the thing I was hired to do." Tulshyan explained that one option, if it's available to you, is "to engage manager support to help [you] push back if requests come from other higher-ups." (I had many of these requests in a previous job.) Tulshyan had other suggestions: "Simply, 'I would love to, but I ordered lunch the last four times. How about we engage Joe to do it?' Again, super hard to prove definitively, but these things add up—when people of color are seen more as the workers rather than the leaders, it impacts our pay, promotion, and general ability to ascend to leadership." I've certainly had opportunities to turn housework into glamour work, but I've also noticed that once these tasks did turn into glamour work, I often suddenly lost the buy-in from my peers or managers who would have preferred that I stayed quiet and in the background doing the housework.

BE AWARE OF COWORKERS
ACTIVELY SABOTAGING YOUR WORK

Another thing you'll have to be aware of is people trying to sabotage your efforts to elevate your own profile at work. One of my worst experiences in a workplace was working alongside someone who was kind and supportive when they spoke to me but who denigrated me and my work when I wasn't around. This person even told people who I regularly worked with that they should avoid working with me and work with this individual instead to, you know, reduce "confusion" on our team. That's a little more than just keeping you relegated to the housework; it's truly toxic behavior. There's no getting around that it's difficult to divvy up the housework and the glamour work equitably—mostly because fairness isn't part of the mental equation for all involved. For fairness to be a team practice, everyone must *want* to work fairly, and you need managers who are willing to step in and make sure that the work is divvied up evenly. In my case, I had a wonderful manager who was empathetic and who emotionally resonated with my concerns, but this person also worked in an environment that encouraged staffers to just settle their differences by being competitive and seeing who came out on top.

THE DRAWBACK OF BEING REASONABLE

Joan Williams brought up an element of a dynamic familiar to me and maybe familiar to you. Citing research by sociologist Cecilia Ridgeway, Williams explained that "low-status groups who know their place at least get the benefit of being seen as reasonable. But if you don't know your place, then you have a 'personality problem.'"

In other words, how you're judged at work sometimes has less to do with your skills, your ideas, and your performance than it does with whether you understand your fit on the team: who you're allowed to be assertive with and who you need to kowtow to. When I left *Lifehacker*, I had been saddled with a new manager who wanted nothing to do with me or my ideas and plans for the future (except for how the manager could hand off these plans to my replacement as a workbook). In trying to navigate the new landscape, I confided in people who I thought would be allies, and I stood up to people who I thought would be receptive to my ideas and would want to implement them. I now realize that all of those people would have preferred that I stayed quiet and, quite frankly, knew my place.

THE TIGHTROPE EFFECT

Williams invented a term for this paradox of doing your best work while also struggling to stay in your lane: the *tightrope effect*. "The technical term is called *prescriptive bias*," Williams told me. "The experiments mostly come out of gender. I call it the Hillary problem or the Serena problem. About ten years ago, I was going, 'Excuse me, this happens by race, too.' If you're an angry Black person, that's not a great career move, regardless of your sex. Now, there are a few experiments that do show that there is a tightrope problem for race because the metaphor is that office politics is more complicated. White men just need to be authoritative and ambitious in order to succeed, but every other group needs to be authoritative and ambitious in a way that's seen as acceptable by white men. That's a lot more complicated. That's walking the tightrope. This office-housework, glamour-work dynamic is part of tightrope bias."

UNDERSTANDING IF YOU HAVE
A WILLING PARTNER IN YOUR BOSS

But how do you work with your manager to assign work fairly? Tulshyan said, "One way to ensure that work is assigned fairly is to keep track of—even if it's writing out—who is doing what. Who was asked to do the glamour work, and who was asked to do the office housework?" If your manager does indicate a willingness to make sure you have glamour opportunities and recognizes the validity of your data showing that you're doing much of the housework while others are getting the glamour work, then you may have a willing partner in your boss. That's really the best you can hope for, assuming that your boss follows through on helping assign work more equitably. Don't just assume your manager is going to change behaviors overnight, though. You'll still need to keep track of who has been assigned what, since the people on your team who are getting the glamour work are not likely to just accept the housework quietly. After all, if someone who has been accustomed to getting all the plum assignments suddenly has to take a turn booking conference rooms and putting together PowerPoint decks for other people, the person may assume the work is beneath them. If that is the case, then their attitude certainly says something about how they viewed you, doesn't it?

"Cultivating awareness and spending time getting educated on how biases show up in the workplace is paramount," Tulshyan said, referring to managers who too often let their own subconscious biases influence who gets what assignments. "It does not come from attending one training, but rather from time spent really getting educated and learning widely on how pervasive workplace bias is. From listening to perspectives different from your own. From knowing this will never be fully done; there's always more to learn. That's how I've caught myself, even in my classroom, to ensure students of color are given opportunities to shine. It takes intention and practice."

MAKE IT EASY FOR YOUR MANAGER TO HELP YOU

Where you'll run into trouble is if your manager isn't terribly interested in doing anything about the unfair distribution of work on your team. Maybe the boss just doesn't want to rock the boat or deal with a problematic colleague who has stopped producing the best work. Maybe your manager empathizes with you but doesn't want to deal with you, either. Whatever the reason, if your manager isn't willing to make changes on their own, you can make some suggestions that might make the decision easier. For example, consider asking to round-robin some of the housework duties, by pointing out things like "Hey, I noticed that I'm always asked to order lunch for the team meetings. I don't mind doing that, but would it be okay if we set up a schedule so everyone has to do it once every month?" Sometimes the difference between managers who are willing to help and those who are reluctant is simply a question of their energy. Instead of bringing them a problem that they should solve, you bring it to them with potential solutions they can use right away. This approach, of course, makes their job easier overall. So suggesting that they take specific action to fix the problem can help. You may also get some traction by bringing your own glamour work ideas to them and asking for their support on your own projects. That way, you're effectively assigning yourself glamour work, although it doesn't remove the housework from your plate, necessarily. But that's another conversation with your manager entirely.

Finally, you could use the housework you've been doing, and your new data, to advocate for yourself in other ways, for example, at your next performance review or the next time you ask for a raise. Telling your manager that you're the one doing the work that effectively is the glue that holds the team together is a great way to say that the team would be way worse off without you and that you're more valuable than you're paid to be. Once you start keeping track of the things you do, the possibilities are endless, and there's something powerful in attending a meeting with your boss and saying, "I'm the only one on our team who knows how to do X, Y, Z, A, B, and C." If they don't consider those things particularly important or high-skill tasks, your boss at least has to reckon with the fact that you're the only one doing this essential work and that you should be properly compensated for it, even if it's not high-profile.

To be sure, hoping managers will assign work equitably isn't a perfect solution, and as I've mentioned earlier, the onus of fixing structural inequality in your workplace, regardless of the reason it exists, shouldn't fall to the person being marginalized. When I sat smiling at passersby at my desk at the *Times* but screaming internally, wondering why I'd been left out of yet another meeting, or having to learn secondhand that someone had worked around me instead of with me, it shouldn't have been my problem to resolve. But the unfortunate reality is that, well, the working world isn't fair, and it probably won't be in the near future. So we have to come up with ways to cope and survive on our own while still maintaining our own personal dignity.

"I also would like more managers to think about how to create more psychological safety on their teams," Tulshyan said. "How often does everyone get to speak up? Are people penalized for risk-taking and sharing ideas? It all adds up. When people of color feel safe, they're more likely to feel supported to push back even if you, as a manager, are assigning them office housework."

Plus, if you can shift mindsets from one where you're under the gun and facing incredible odds to one where your struggle is proof of your strength and resilience, you can—as I did—turn that simmering anger and resentment into the fuel you need to propel yourself to greater heights in your career. You will learn to never settle until you find an environment that's right for you and you're surrounded by people who respect and appreciate you.

Figure Out
Your Unique Contribution

(BEING A SUPERSTAR)

For a long time, my professional goal at every job was to make sure I was a superstar, as in an employee who has the essential skills that other people on your team may not have. A superstar is indispensable to the point where you're not only needed but also respected and in demand. And of course, I wanted to be a superstar to make myself *extremely* difficult to fire or lay off. I didn't necessarily need to do glamour work, as I discussed earlier, but I did the kind of work that made me indispensable to the team. That is, my employer would literally have to hire someone to do what I knew how to do, and without doing that, it would need to keep me around. When I was a fourteen-year-old at my first job ever, working retail, I predictably decided to be the guy you could always call to pick up a shift and who was the fastest checkout scanner there, the one with the line that people wanted to get in. That energy got me promoted to service desk manager, which was really not so much a promotion but an acknowledgment that my cheery demeanor made me good with customers. My employer put me where I'd have to deal with customers more and scan and bag items less. The new position made me flexible and able to cover shifts all over the store, and it certainly made me valuable enough that I could quit to go back to school and come back to open arms and plenty of hours during summer breaks.

When I worked in information technology, I decided to be the cross-platform guy, the one who was certified to work on both PCs and Macs. The role earned me a pretty nice assignment with the then director of the neuro-oncology branch of the National Cancer Institute. He would call and ask for me directly when he had computer problems, and he and his staff trusted me to handle his needs—so much so that they were all dismayed when I eventually moved on to another job. (I still miss those folks, though; they were all really nice and appreciated my work.)

When I was a project manager, being a superstar meant not just being cheerful or holding special skills but also being the only person with the strategic knowledge of every cog and wheel of a given project. Of course, that's part of the job description, and it didn't hurt that I was the only project manager on the team. (I was fiercely resistant when my then CIO wanted to hire a director of project management to oversee my efforts: What if the director didn't like the way I did things? What if this individual hire didn't think I was as valuable as I thought I was? Of course, he was hired anyway, we became friends, and I learned a lot from working with him, so I had nothing to worry about. But you understand why I *would* be worried.)

But being the only project manager on the team meant that I was a locus of information—the person everyone turned to in order to figure out what was happening next, how much time they had to do their tasks, and how much time would be required to make an idea come to life. I was the person who got to see the smiles of my superiors when I told them that their ambitious idea could be done in the time frame they wanted. I was also the person who let them down when it couldn't be done, but I offered the olive branch of sitting down and talking about what we *could* do in the time we had. Most of this proficiency came down to my being collaborative and willing to work with people and understanding that their goals are often my shared goals and that we could and should find success together.

SUPERSTAR SOFT SKILLS

So being a superstar is essential to get respect and be in demand enough that you get the glamour work and the projects you want to work on. But how do you become known as one? How do you go from being a cog in the machine to the kind of person who managers would hate to lay off or lose to a competitor if another job offer came knocking on your door? How do you become the employee whose name carries some leverage in making sure you get another job if you're ever laid off or your company falls out from under you? I asked Adam Grant, organizational psychologist, professor at the Wharton School, and author of incredible books like *Give and Take: A Revolutionary Approach to Success, Originals: How Non-Conformists Move the World,* and *Think Again: The Power of Knowing What You Don't Know,* as well as the host of the *WorkLife* podcast, what he thought. "I think it's still true that in most workplaces, the way that people maintain their job security is through their competence and their contribution," he told me. "People get to keep their jobs if they're seen as having unique skills and using those skills in a way that makes the team or the organization better. Or even just makes the boss look *good*.

"I think if you take that idea seriously, that means a lot of people would define those narrowly in terms of technical skills, but I think that increasingly we're starting to see hard data for the value of soft skills, right? Being somebody who is unusually proactive and excellent at judging when to take initiative and when to not immediately reply to an email because it's going to then dump a task that your manager just crossed off their list back onto their list."

It's difficult to overstate those soft skills that Grant described. Sure, it's one thing to be the expert, as I was the Apple guy, but it also really helps to be the person who foresees the problems that only you can solve quickly and who can offer the solutions required to get everyone back to work. It also helps to be the person who the team can rely on for a specific thing but also to be likable enough to work with so that people want to rely on you for help, as opposed to groaning when they need your specialized skills. "I think there's increasing recognition of the value of anticipating the problems that are going to need to be solved and then trying to get a leg up on them," Grant told me. "We could go through a whole list of those kinds of qualities, but I think you're asking something really important that's been understudied and underappreciated in performance and productivity research, which is it's just easier for some people to get credit for their expertise.

"In my world of organizational psychology, I think we've done a much better job on gender than we have on race. I think in a lot of cases, it's a question of being a member of a nondominant group and saying, 'Look, if you're not a white man, then you're just less likely to have your competence taken for granted and you're more likely to have to prove it over and over and over again, which is grossly unfair.'"

Much of becoming a superstar starts with mindset, with determination. And that's especially important for marginalized employees and employees of color, who have to deal with, again, the social baggage that comes with their identities at the office. Personally, as a Black man, I've had to turn up the charm often and keep a smile on my face. I've done it for so long—across multiple jobs and for many, many years—that more than a few people recognize me by my smile and have commented that they're always happy to see my face smiling at them, no matter what's going on in the world or how their day may be going. I mean, I *am* a generally cheerful person, and I like to think that I do have a smile for everyone I meet, but don't think for a second that I don't understand exactly how important it is for a Black male in America to be as nonthreatening as possible to the people around him. My very survival is at stake. All it takes is one dour glance at the wrong moment to the wrong person, and they're on the phone with emergency services, claiming they fear for their life and they want the police to protect them from me as soon as possible. That's the kind of scenario that can end up with my death.

So for marginalized workers, being a superstar is partly about having the right mindset and excelling at the work, but it's also about playing a part many of us have been playing our entire lives. Not only do you need to meet the qualifications of *adequate* to be viewed in the same ballpark as your privileged colleagues, but you also need to outshine them at everything you do—and stay humble while you do it. It's the only way to make sure your qualifications and your space in the room aren't challenged.

COUNTERING THE STEREOTYPE
OF WHAT A LEADER LOOKS LIKE

Grant and I discussed Ashleigh Rosette's research, specifically in her paper "The White Standard," with regard to how and when your qualifications are seen either as worthy of promotion or as the default at best or challengeable at worst.[1] In short, Rosette explains that part of the reason it's so difficult for people of color or anyone else in a marginalized group to succeed at work is because our prototypical view of what makes a leader is generally a white, cisgender, able-bodied young man. This "leader" has no disability, is not discriminated against because of his ethnicity, and so on. He's a boilerplate white male, and if you don't match that description, you're going to seem out of place, no matter how you look at it.

"There's this tendency," Grant explained, "especially if you're thinking, 'Okay, I'm a superstar at my individual contributor job and I want to move up,' there's likely to be a mismatch between you and what people are by default expecting in the role if you're not a white dude. As a result, you have to work that much harder to prove yourself. You have to work that much harder to counteract a lot of the stereotypes that are held of a leader. Then you have to be doubly careful because we expect leaders to be dominant and assertive but watch out if you're a Black man trying to be dominant and assertive."

So understanding that there is a stereotype of what a leader looks like, you should move beyond this issue, which you can't do anything about, and work on becoming a subject-matter expert at your work or in your field: the person everyone turns to for specialized help. This role can be especially difficult, because being the team member everyone seeks out for expert assistance also means you can quickly become the person who's always asked to help with other people's work. This role, while valuable, can mean doing the housework that no one else wants to do or knows how to do.

I ran into this quandary at the *New York Times*. I was so eager to prove myself and get involved to show my peers that I had valuable skills to bring to the table that I eventually wound up taking on some regular editing duties for another team. I was grateful for the opportunity, and the editor who let me help him out is a wonderful person and was doing it out of admiration for my skills. What's more, I was eager for a chance to help out. He eventually moved on to another role, as did his manager, who was also eager to have my contribution on their team. After they departed, I kept going as before because I knew people were relying on me to do what I knew how to do best. I never got the feeling that my work wasn't appreciated, and I definitely felt like the person who, everyone on the team thought, "knew how to do what I do best."

However, over time, when management changed and new faces were in charge, it was clear that what I was working on was, to them at least, more of a checkbox that needed ticking and, while valuable, not too important. So instead of being the expert who helped and taught others to do what I knew how to do, I became the housekeeper who came in every few weeks to do a thing, was thanked, and was summarily ignored or dismissed the rest of the time. It was unfortunate, but I didn't *dislike* the work I was doing. It did take a lot for me to stand up for myself and say, "Hey, I was supposed to be helping out," and eventually move on to the next project.

LEARN TO SET YOUR BOUNDARIES

Adam Grant had some wise words about this scenario as well, and for most people, it comes back around to a classic piece of advice: "I think you probably need boundaries around who you help and when you help and how you help. I saw this a lot in my research on givers and takers: that people who sort of became a doormat or who got reputations for helping out, as opposed to the strategic or visible or glamorous, they tended to say yes to all the people all the time with all the requests. What that meant for their reputation was they were known as nice people who you could dump any grunt task on." His description sure sounded familiar, and I immediately thought of my own role on that team, when the colleagues who truly appreciated me left and were replaced with people who only saw me as a resource they could use.

FIGURE OUT WHAT YOUR
UNIQUE CONTRIBUTION LOOKS LIKE

Grant explained how people can set boundaries: "I think what successful givers do on average is they set boundaries and they say, 'I'm going to help in ways that actually add real value.' That means I'm going to try to align what I say yes to with the team's mission, with the organization's mission, with what people in power actually need and care about."

He continued: "They also are more likely to set boundaries if somebody had a history or reputation of selfish behavior, and say, 'Look, I'm not going to reward a taker for exploiting me. I'm going to reserve my contributions for people who pay it back and pay it forward.' They tended to block out time to get their own work done so that they didn't get stuck doing everybody else's job and fall behind on their own productivity. I guess that's a time management skill, whereas the first one was more emotional intelligence. Then they also tended to become specialists instead of generalists, and I think this is the most interesting part—to say, 'All right. Let me figure out what I can contribute that's unique to me that other people can't.'"

And that's the key. Having those special skills is one thing, but at the same time, you have to know how to apply your skills, and when.

That's just one example of how being a subject-matter expert helps you get so far, but it's no replacement for being respected and appreciated. So be wary of helping, because all too often, especially for women and workers of color, we're expected to help out whenever and wherever it's needed, to show that we're good team players or have initiative. And we're also more likely to jump at those opportunities to prove ourselves, even if we don't necessarily have to. In short, choose your helping-out opportunities carefully. Base your decision on who is asking for your help. How well do you know them? If they will truly appreciate your efforts and vouch for you when the chips are down, then you know they're someone you can invest time and energy into helping.

HOW TO SAY YES WHEN
YOU WANT TO TAKE ON A PROJECT

On a personal level, I hate that office relationships have to be this transactional. (And in reality, not all of them do; sometimes it's great to lend a helping hand to a colleague or another team just for the benefit of doing so.) But you absolutely have to take the steps to defend your time and energy when you're already busy, struggling with prioritization, and trying to be productive when you're bringing the social baggage of your identity to work every day. The last thing you want to do is try to sort out whether someone wants your help because they really do respect your time and your expertise or because they have some busywork that needs to get done and they wouldn't want to saddle their white, male superstar with it. The following sections present some simple ways to defend your time and energy when you're faced with a request.

Never say yes immediately. Don't agree to a project unless you're absolutely certain you want to. You must decouple any energetic desire to prove yourself or to feel like a part of the team from the logic center of your brain for a moment. If you are certain that someone is extending an olive branch that will turn into glamour work or that you'll be in a position to do something really special with the task you're being asked to help out with, then sure, go for it. But if you're not sure what you're signing up for or how long your help will be needed, then tell your colleague—even if it's a manager or another superior—that you need to give it some thought. Tell them you're really flattered that they asked you, and that you'll need to check on what you have going on at the moment to make sure that you can do their project justice. It's a fair delay and one that will give you time to think things through.

Understand the time commitment. Don't make any snap decisions. I know it's tough to slow down, even after you've said that you'll get back to the person, but a mistake I made in the past was not negotiating exactly how I would help and for how long. When the wonderful folks I was working with were promoted or moved on and I was still there "helping," I should have had a lever to pull to say, "Okay, I'll leave you with some notes on what I've learned and go back to my regular duties on X date." I didn't have that lever, so make sure that you do. Whatever the side project is—for example, a presentation at an industry conference (which has a built-in end date) or an ongoing engagement where you're "embedded" with another team (which could go on forever)—you should always consider exactly how much of your time and energy this is going to consume. You should also consider whether you have the time and energy to give. Finally, find out when, exactly, you will be finished with this side work and can return triumphantly to your regular job and responsibilities, having accomplished something great that you can add to your résumé. If the assignment doesn't sound like it will play out that way, either make sure it does, or say no.

Check in with your manager. The biggest mistake you can make when you say yes to something is to do so without asking your supervisor. So don't take that stint helping out another department without at least letting your manager know that you'd like to do it.

Note that I said "that you'd like to do it," not "that you were asked." There's nuance here when it comes to different kinds of managers: If you have a good boss, they'll want to be in the loop on everything so they understand how much work you're doing and how thinly stretched you may be before they ask you to do something for them. Others are just territorial and will balk at the notion of someone else asking one of their "resources" to do something they may or may not approve of. And on one level, that's completely fair—your manager may have a tight handle on your bandwidth and the things you need to do. So someone else's cruising in and demanding a chunk of your time that could otherwise be devoted to your own team and your collective goals is a slight at best and an intentional poaching at worst. That's why you must first decide whether you want to do this work, before you even check in with your manager. For all you know, the other person may have already checked with your boss to make sure it was okay to ask you. Either way, make sure you go into that conversation with your own desires ready to go. The last thing you want to do is leave the decision up to your boss—a mistake I've made before—when you should be responsible for your own direction. Be open to talking things through with your boss if they disagree, of course, but it will help if you go in with what you want first.

Say no without ruining your career. This is the tough part. Saying yes is easy—but it's ultimately the most costly decision you can make. If the situation just isn't a good match for you or if the work will take up more time and energy than you know you can spare, or if your manager isn't on board but would support whatever decision you make, maybe it's best to just say no. But it's never as easy as just saying, "I'm too busy," especially if you're already marginalized, and even more so if that person is in a position of authority. Declining is still an option, though. You just have to be tactful about it. This is where keeping track of what you're working on and who's being assigned what work is really important. If you have an idea of what's already on your plate, you can look any manager in the eye and say, "I just don't have the bandwidth right now. I have X, Y, Z, A, B, and C on my plate, and they really do take up all of my time." If it's something you wish you could help with but know it's not going to work out, say something like "I'd really love to help, but I just don't have the time right now with everything else going on. Can we check back in maybe X months and I'll see if I can lend a hand then?"

THE POWER OF "NO, BUT"

The well-known "no, but" phrase, which translates as "I won't do it, but there are conditions or circumstances that would change my mind," is infinitely more powerful than you might think. It's a helpful place to retreat to if you know that there's a power differential between you and the person asking and you don't want to just rebuff them. It's also helpful if you actually would like to help, but you don't want the time you'd spend helping someone else to mean you working tons of overtime just to make sure your normal work doesn't slip through the cracks. Even a little flattery can go a long way: "Thanks for thinking of me! I'll have to pass, though. I have a lot going on at the moment, but we can catch up later and maybe I can help out then!" That response is one of my favorites. It's firm, it points out that you're in control of your own workflow, but it also expresses genuine happiness that the person considered you for whatever opportunity it is, even if that opportunity is pretty shitty.

"NOT THIS, BUT THAT"

Grant also had advice on how to be a superstar and how to make yourself a subject-matter expert (and how to be careful about picking where you apply those skills). He said that instead of just saying no, you'll want to communicate "not this, but that," when presented with work that's not a good fit for your skills or your goals.

"When somebody comes to me with something that doesn't fit," he explained, "I'm going to say, 'You know what, that's actually not my expertise,' or 'I'm actually stretched in the following directions, but if you need help in these ways, let me know.' What that seems to signal is, one, I have expertise and, two, I'm not a jerk. I'm willing to help. It's just that you didn't come to me with the right request."

FLEXIBILITY ON YOUR OWN TERMS

There's another benefit to managing your own workload and being selective about the extra work you accept. It comes back to proving that you're a superstar—or at least an essential employee where you work. Your judiciousness and self-management show everyone that you're acutely aware of what you have on your plate and what you can and cannot accomplish within a certain time. You're in a position to say things like "I don't think I have time to do the entire task right now, but what if I got you Y by your deadline? Would that work for you?" One of my most powerful tools when I was a project manager was staring down someone's absolutely unworkable deadline—knowing that it was impossible and knowing that *they knew* it was impossible—and saying, "Listen, I don't think this timeline makes sense, but what are the most important things we can deliver by that deadline to buy us time to do the rest?" Flexibility is a sorely underrated skill. Although marginalized employees, including people of color, have to be flexible to keep their jobs, they can use that flexibility as a tool to manage their own work rather than as a tool to meet someone else's demands. This approach is a great way to keep cool at work while showing everyone around you that you're capable of long-term, big-picture thinking.

After all, the ability to see the big picture, adjust your schedule and workload when necessary, and plan for your team's needs is what separates great employees from average ones. And when the chips are already down because your workplace rewards the loudest man in the room or where, regardless of your skills and background, no one thinks you belong, you need all the help you can get.

TRANSFORM WORK INTO SOMETHING
YOU TAKE AN ACTIVE ROLE IN

Taking the time to review your work is one big way to help yourself. Later, I'll discuss how to make a productivity system that works well for you, but at this stage, you may have noticed that a lot of what it takes to be a superstar at work is less about doing hard things and being good at them and more about knowing when to chip in and when to bow out. It's also about knowing when to go all in on being the hero who saves the day and when to step back and be the strategist who can see all the trains on all the tracks and make sure they all arrive safely. Being a superstar is more than just doing housework or checking boxes off a job description: It's high-level, executive-style work. It's leadership. And it's work that, on some level, you're probably already doing every day. The only difference—and this difference is key in this book—is to transform your work from something you do in your own head, eyes lowered and convinced that it is something you have to passively endure, into something you actively take a role in. You turn your work into something you deliberately manage and for which you learn to set professional goals and politely but firmly set your own personal boundaries.

And speaking of learning to say no to bosses, Grant pointed out that there's something special to consider when it comes to this challenging task. "Everybody has at some point been a victim of either a taker boss or a toxic leader who is abusive and taking advantage of them. And it's not so easy to say no when you report to that person." He said that one way to get out of this difficult situation is to reduce your dependence on that person. You can try to shift the reporting arrangement, change bosses, or start looking for another role. The other way, Grant said, is to "increase their dependence on you so that when you truly are indispensable, they become a little bit more careful about abusing you, because they don't want to lose you or undermine the quality of your work."

This strong dependence is an awkward arrangement but worth keeping in mind, especially if your relationship with your manager isn't the best or if you lack the psychological safety with your boss to expect their support if you tell them that you've been marginalized. "I think, on the one hand, that's an effective strategy," Grant said. But he warned that "it's also a dangerous strategy because you don't want to be so indispensable to somebody above you that you can never get promoted or rotated into a new assignment for learning and development opportunities. Short term, helpful. Long term, potentially very dangerous."

DON'T BE AFRAID TO PRAISE YOUR OWN WORK

Doing good work that you're proud of and only taking on work that you know you can excel at is just the start of the race. The next part is learning not to be afraid to praise your own work. Keep in mind that many people in any workplace are more than happy to advocate for themselves—and haven't been socialized not to. These folks will take one praising email from a customer and forward it to their entire team, their boss, their boss's boss, that person's boss, and on up the chain, just to say, "See? Our customers *love* what I've been doing!"

When I was the editor in chief of *Lifehacker*, before the management changes, the bankruptcy, and the lawsuit and before everything fell apart, I used to enjoy hanging out with my bosses. I'd wander over to where John Cook, Adam Pash, and Lacey Donohue sat, plop right down on the couch behind them, and beg their advice and opinion as people who had been in leadership positions at the org for years longer than I had. Pash had once been in the same role—editor in chief of *Lifehacker*—and he was the one who had hired me long before then, as a staff writer, in the first place. He also advocated for my promotion to editor in chief, as did Cook and Donohue. I was determined to do his judgment justice, and I wanted to make all three of them proud, since they had all advocated for me to take the top job. Those conversations were learning experiences, and I distinctly remember one where I caught Lacey on her own, likely defusing some smoldering fire that one of us had started at one of the many publications under her command. I asked her why *Lifehacker* (one of several websites owned by the parent company, Gawker Media) hung in the background so often, when we were so integral to the team and did so much for the company. She said it was because we had a history of being a team that was too comfortable working on the sidelines and that I was no exception. She urged me to advocate for myself more often—to speak up when I wanted something, especially if I had an idea that I knew would do well. She confided that she knew other editors who wound up getting the things they asked for simply because they were noisier about asking—not necessarily because their ideas were better or because they were more talented or experienced, but because they were better at advocating for themselves and their teams.

I took her comments to heart. Of course, self-promotion doesn't always work, because when you advocate for yourself, some people are willing to listen to your accomplishments and believe that you can do what you say you can do, but other people are not so willing. Suffice it to say that before my last days at *Lifehacker*, I had to advocate for myself and my team in front of someone who didn't believe in me or my expertise or skills at all. And when the negotiation came down to "you or your team," I chose my team and walked away. But since then, I've been in a number of positions where I was the only person who *would* advocate for myself. For example, at the *New York Times*, an infamously competitive environment, only the most major successes were shared. Everyone else had to learn to toot their own horn, as it were, at least on the team I was on. When I saw my colleagues emailing our managers with their successes, I learned that if I wanted to even be a blip on their radar as someone doing good work and worth hiring in the first place, I'd have to do the same. And frankly, that's not totally uncalled-for. It's safe to assume that your boss, and your boss's boss, are probably busy doing their own jobs, and that while good managers do check in with their employees, a written record of a win or a major accomplishment is sometimes a great help when they go looking for something to discuss in your next performance review.

IT'S UP TO YOU TO TELL YOUR BOSS ABOUT YOUR ACHIEVEMENTS

And of course, for those of us who are marginalized at work either because of race or ethnicity, as I was, or because of some other issue that sets you apart from the majority in your workplace, you're already in a position where others see you as your identity and not your skills or accomplishments. Sadly, because of their narrower view, we tend to keep our heads down and stay quiet, hoping that the good work we do will shine through and people will see it. Let me disabuse you of that notion right now: They won't. Not without you telling them, and not without them actively being on the lookout for it. So it's up to you to make sure your boss knows when you're doing good things, when you've wrapped up a big project successfully, or when you've earned a big win, in whatever form that may take for your job. You have to be the person who emails your boss and tells them about the milestone you just crossed or offers to send weekly wrap-ups where you highlight the great things you accomplished that week. You don't have to be so transparent that anyone could tell the emails were self-aggrandizing and conceited. In fact, it's more effective if you're *not* that kind of person. But even if you meet your boss one-on-one armed with a list of your latest accomplishments you'd like to share, it's better than hoping your boss will notice on their own.

Also, finding others in the workplace who can identify with you and support your ideas and your work goes a long way toward having people who look forward to working with you and are willing to sing your praises. As you keep track of your work, highlight your accomplishments and share them with people who are willing to support your ideas. You'll soon find that people will consider you a subject-matter expert. It always helps to have other people in your corner, even if they are not on your team or don't work directly with you. They can tell others how valuable you are and talk up your knowledge and skills that may be underutilized. These folks will look out for you if things go badly, and they're the

ones you should be more likely to say yes to when they come calling for your help.

SOMETIMES, BEING A SUPERSTAR ISN'T ENOUGH

But here's the other side of the learning-to-be-a-superstar coin, one
that's critical for marginalized workers to understand. This observation especially applies not just to workers of color, but also to workers with disabilities, visible or otherwise; women working in all-male
offices; or even workers who have chronic illness or mental health
issues that their employer knows about, even if it doesn't affect their
work in the slightest. Ready?

Not even being an essential worker can always help you overcome institutional racism or preconceived notions about cultural fit.
Sometimes you can do everything right and it still isn't enough.
Here's why: In workplaces dominated by any single group of
people—whether it's an old-boys' club and the only folks who are
respected have Ivy League degrees, or it's a women's club where all
the diversity and inclusion positions seem to be filled by white
women, who then continue to hire white women for other roles in
the organization—that majority is going to judge you primarily on
how well you fit into that singular group. You may be able to get by
because you're great at what you do. You can talk the talk and code-
switch, setting aside elements of your personality—your language,
manner of speaking, and even your demeanor—to fit in with the
group of people you're around at work. You can even be so essential
in your position that no one else does what you do or knows what
you know.

But you're still an outsider. You won't be one of the in group, precisely because of that fundamental difference between you and everyone else, whatever that difference may be. And it's not because you didn't try, either, or because you're unwilling to be friendly. In many cases, that pressure to keep you at arm's length comes from inside the room. People use your difference as a justification for keeping you on the outside. Sure, they'd love to be friends with you, boost your profile, and show you the respect and appreciation that you deserve, but you're just not "a fit" or, worse, not "a cultural fit."

When I left my role as the editor in chief at *Lifehacker*, essentially released without cause, I was told that it was because the management team was "looking for something new and different." No one told me what that new and different was, and no one told me where I'd fallen down on the job. In fact, I had recently received glowing performance reviews and had happily (although expensively) moved to New York City to settle into the leadership of then Gawker media, *Lifehacker*'s parent organization at the time. But a highly publicized legal battle and a sudden bankruptcy later, and the organization had new ownership at the hands of Univision. The new owner would eventually tire of *Lifehacker* and the entire endeavor of running a digital media company and offload it to the lowest bidder, which eventually turned out to be a private equity firm, Great Hill Partners, for a fraction of its worth. But before any of that happened, the newly appointed CEO of Gizmodo Media Group (the new company name after we were forced to shutter Gawker proper) booked me one Wednesday afternoon for a sudden meeting the next day. My main impression of him at this point was as the guy who had a habit of always greeting me last when I'd talk with him in a group.

As I liked to stay late at the office (the peace and quiet helped me work), I popped into his office on my way out to ask if everything was okay, since the meeting seemed to come out of the blue. He gave me a wry smile and said, "We'll talk about it tomorrow." As I walked out of the office, I knew that the following day would be my last. I went home and put my emergency plan into action (we'll get to yours at the end of the book). I made calls to friends, wrote some emails to contacts, and made sure to line up what I needed to ensure that if I went down, I wouldn't be down long. And sure enough, the following day was my last there. The only senior editor of color the publication had ever had and, to my knowledge, one of an astonishingly small number in the organization as a whole, past or present.

That was the moment when it crystallized for me that just being good at what I do—being diligent, holding institutional knowledge, knowing things that other people don't, and working well with the people around me—wasn't going to be enough to save me. I landed on my feet at the *Times,* but that did not lessen the pain and humiliation that comes with building something with love and passion for years only to be told that you're not good enough for it.

At the end of the day, the company you work for and the managers you report to are not your friends, even if they ostensibly think they are, and sometimes being a superstar at work means you have to cozy up to people and feel as if you're making friends, when you're not. In more ways than one, I wish I'd learned that sooner.

YOU HAVE TO TRY ANYWAY

I know what you are asking: If you can bend over backward, give your absolute all, and make yourself vulnerable both personally and professionally to become a superstar in your field or at your job, and none of it really matters and all of it can be ripped from you in an instant—why should you bother making an effort?

Well, the moral is that you have to try anyway. You have to bring your A game at all times, and you have to do your absolute best. You have to make yourself as essential as possible, because for marginalized workers and especially workers of color, becoming difficult to replace is the first step toward becoming essential. And once you're essential, you may eventually be recognized as an expert in your field or craft, so that slowly but surely, the people at your workplace will come to respect you for who you are and what you do. And those people will be there to make sure that your light never goes out. They'll reach for you, and you should make sure to reach back. That's the real network—the real in group—and it may include people who are marginalized the same way you are or people who are just perceptive and understand exactly what you're capable of.

That's what it really means to be a superstar. It's not so much specific job protection or even industry protection. It's about becoming the kind of person for whom your professional and personal credibility and accomplishments all resonate further than you think that they do, and with people you may not even know. The goal is to transcend any particular job or company, so you'll always have an opportunity to do what only you can do.

Be a Problem Solver,
Not a Problem Complainer

(MANAGING UP)

A lot of advice—especially to marginalized people, including those who have been actively discriminated against by their coworkers, comes in the form of "talk to your manager." Or in other cases, "talk to your HR department." It sounds good in theory to get on the record what you're going through, even if you don't name names and don't tell all. At least you make it clear to the powers that be that something is wrong and you have set boundaries around what kind of behavior you'll tolerate and what kind you won't.

Unfortunately, not all managers are interested in addressing issues on their teams, whether the problems relate to an employee's bad behavior or an employee who feels constantly left out of the opportunities they're qualified to take on. Nor are all HR departments interested in the fair treatment of their workers and the diversity of their teams. Many departments opt instead to work as arms of the company's legal department to make sure there are no complaints or other problems and especially nothing that could expose the company to any kind of risk. So of course, you do need to be careful when you're talking about bringing your concerns up with your manager or your company's HR department. In some cases, doing so will help get your concerns addressed. In other cases, it will turn out poorly for you and may end with either a planned or an unplanned exit from the company.

PSYCHOLOGICAL SAFETY IS YOUR FIRST PRIORITY

So what do you do, then? Let's start with your manager. Consider your relationship with this person and their receptivity to what you've told them in the past. You probably already have an idea of whether your manager will take anything you say seriously or, better yet, whether they'll actually work with you on fixing a problem you have in the workplace, even if that problem is difficult. For now, we'll assume that you have a manager you think would be willing to work with you or at least be open to listening to your concerns. Next, you have to consider whether you, personally, have the psychological safety to open up to them about it. I've mentioned psychological safety earlier in the book, but to put a finer point on it, a person who feels psychologically safe with a boss feels able to tell them about a problem and trust that the boss will consider the person's feelings and discuss perspectives truthfully and openly. You may have a boss who's willing to help, but if you think they wouldn't understand your concerns, then you don't have the psychological safety to bring those issues up.

For example, let's say you have a disability and believe that your teammates are excluding you from happy hours and other events because they get tired of you asking them about the location. You just want to be able to decide if you'd be comfortable there, and you bring up the issue to your boss. It's one thing to have a boss who will say, "That's awful, but they probably just don't know and you can do that research yourself." It's another to have a boss who will affirm your concerns and say, "That's awful. I'll make sure that every place we book for events and off-sites has accessibility options." See the difference? And you, as the person with the issue, probably already have some innate sense of whether your manager will reply with understanding, reply with understanding *and* affirmation, or reject you entirely. That's the level of psychological safety you have to gauge before you do anything.

If you feel you do have that level of safety, then congratulations, your boss is likely to openly listen and discuss what you and they can do to make the situation better, if there is anything. If you don't feel that psychological safety, but you do think your boss may listen, there are still some things you can do to make your voice and your concerns heard.

I sat down with Katherine Crowley and Kathi Elster, the previously mentioned authors of several excellent books on navigating office culture and the unspoken rules of dealing with managers. Their works include the titles *Working with You Is Killing Me, Working for You Isn't Working for Me,* and *Mean Girls at Work* and, most recently, the podcast *My Crazy Office,* which they host. We talked about how to manage up and how marginalized workers can make sure their managers are effective allies.

MEET WITH YOUR BOSS REGULARLY

"The first thing is, you have got to get your boss to meet with you regularly," Elster told me. "When we say *meet*, we don't mean as they are leaving the room or as they are hanging up or running to the next thing. We're talking about actually having locked out time for you to meet with your boss, because if the boss is distracted or busy doing other things, they're not going to remember a thing you say. You have to train your boss because many bosses just don't want to give their staff the time. If you book it and then they cancel it, rebook it. You have to be willing to do that."

Elster's observations could have been ripped from my own experience. I've had several managers who, not to their fault exactly, were like me in a way: Meeting is a pain, and skipping meetings is great! If you can give back to your boss some time to actually get work done, isn't that a good thing? Sure—as long as both you and your boss are on the same page about your work and as long as you believe they're effectively advocating for you and assigning work fairly. If not, however, you need to check in with them regularly to make sure that they do support you. Several of my managers would regularly cancel our one-on-ones because they believed they had nothing to discuss, they wanted to give me the time back, or they were so busy they always seemed to have a conflict. I should have followed up for a different time to meet, especially for the managers who I believed could have helped if I had talked through my concerns with them.

IT'S A CHALLENGE, BUT DON'T TAKE
BEING MARGINALIZED PERSONALLY

Those meetings don't have to be long, Crowley said. "Even fifteen minutes," she explained, is enough. "It's the thing of getting airtime, and it's interesting that when you're talking about being marginalized, it can be very challenging not to take it personally if you set up a meeting and then you're blown off," she said. "It's one of those things where you actually need to not take it personally and persevere because I think a big part of being marginalized is that you're not fully seen; you're not fully known. This is so essential in terms of changing your experience."

While Crowley, Elster, and I were talking, I thought back to the times when I did feel invisible in my organizations. At times, I labored in silence, churning out work that I was arguably proud of and that my manager seemed happy with, but I still felt as if I were spinning my wheels. In hindsight, what I often took for freedom, flexibility, and the opportunity to chart my own course was sometimes indeed partly that. But looking at it in another light, I had also been set adrift, with little to no tether to shore. Was this lack of guidance my managers' fault? They might have been partly responsible, because they could have been more hands-on with their management or at least more supportive of my work. But neither did I reach out. I wound up feeling marginalized, which then led to a cycle of self-marginalization, which is never good.

MAKE SURE YOU COME TO THE MEETING
WITH AN AGENDA

The second major tenet of learning to manage up is to make sure you come to those meetings with an agenda—even a checklist of things you want to talk to your manager about, like fair work assignments or those glamour opportunities that you'd like to get (or didn't get). "Of course, these days, it'll be digital," Crowley said. "That's fine, but you should have it and you should also share it with your boss. That document becomes your lifesaver because it helps you prioritize what it is you should be working on. It helps you take notes about what you and the boss agree on as far as next steps are concerned." Crowley explained that this is exceptionally helpful for different kinds of managers: The forgetful manager will get a jogged memory when you show them the agenda and your notes from the previous one-on-one.

KEEP AN EYE ON
YOUR BOSS'S CHANGING PRIORITIES

The third major element of managing up is to keep an eye on your boss's changing priorities. "It's not so much your priorities," Elster explained. "It's that you have to understand that the problem is with your boss." She said that being on top of the boss's priorities could be a daily task: "You always have to understand what's going on in their world. If you understand their changing priorities, then yours should change based on that." But that sounds like a whole second job, I thought, and one that you may not even have much insight into! Before I could even bring up that point, Elster saw where I was going. "Now, many people hate that," she said. "They don't want to ask the boss, 'Hey, have priorities changed today?' because they see it as more work rather than the right work. So they avoid that, but it's really, really critical."

This is advice many of us could use early in our careers, when we're getting comfortable with working in environments where we may not have vision into the shifting winds of middle or upper management. What may be a quiet project one day could suddenly become a serious issue the next because the wrong person got involved or because an executive is paying attention. By the time that information trickles down to you, you might have difficulty dealing with it. The slow communication may be no one's fault, really (except the person or executive who changed the priorities, of course), but if you stay tuned into your boss's priorities, you're likely to encounter fewer surprises. Learning to communicate effectively with your manager about things like that will take you a long way in any job. This skill will change your relationship with your manager from one that's usually adversarial to one that's a bit more collaborative. Make no mistake, I'm not saying your boss has to be—or even will be—your friend if you make these moves or that they'll be less inclined to lay you off or fire you if they're told to do so. But keeping in close communication with your manager does at least make your time working together more seamless. Ultimately, seeing your boss's name in your in-box will be less of a cause for panic or anxiety if you two have a more collegial, collaborative relationship.

ANTICIPATE PROBLEMS

"You always have to anticipate problems and offer solutions," Elster explained, moving on to the next element of managing up. She described someone she recently spoke with. "He's got a really important job in an organization. He is in charge of security at a retirement community. Because of COVID right now, security is, like, 'Don't let people in. Take their temperature'—the whole thing."

Crowley jumped in, grinning. "The problem was, he couldn't believe that there were people who were going to complain at the gatehouse about it." Elster laughed and said, "About having to go through it." Crowley nodded and agreed, and I was shocked. The COVID-19 pandemic had been nearly a year long then, and there was no reason that the residents' complaints should have been new to the security professional in question. People had been complaining about temperature checks and masks in public places in the United States for months, so the response at this retirement center should have been no surprise to him—and he should have predicted it, in my opinion. But like many problems that start small and turn major, maybe he just missed it, or it's just a gap in his professional awareness.

When I suggested that the security person might have just had this one oversight, Crowley said that there were other problems. "There were other things," she said. "Like, he also didn't anticipate that the battery is going to die in the thermometers. He didn't know how to normalize predictable problems. This makes you very valuable to any manager: that you are able to predict what problems are going to occur and then offer solutions so that you don't create problems that are predictable." In short, you need to be less surprised when predictable problems occur and more able to produce solutions to those problems when they happen, if not before.

"You want to be seen as a problem solver, not a problem complainer," Crowley explained.

ALWAYS BE PREPARED TO GIVE A STATUS REPORT

And there's one last important element of managing up—one that we will discuss in detail in Rule 11, about the fine art of looking busy. It's to always, always have something to say if someone asks you what you're working on or how your work is going. "Always be prepared to give a status report," Crowley said. "Most people hate this one as well because it means that you actually have to have a good finger on where you are with any one of the projects that you are currently working on. When your boss comes to you and says, 'What's the status on X, Y, and Z?' you don't know who's asking your boss for that status."

Notably, most of us think so rarely beyond our relationship with our own direct manager that we forget that our boss may be asking us for updates because someone's asking them for updates on what their team is doing or how a project they've assigned to you is coming along.

"Their job depends on you being informed and able to tell them where things stand," Crowley said, referring to your relationship with your manager. Elster chimed in: "People often see that as 'They don't trust me; they're checking up on me,' when actually, no, somebody asked them for the information, and who else are they going to go to for information? It's amazing how many people don't get that."

ASSUME YOUR BOSS DOESN'T REALLY KNOW ALL THAT MUCH ABOUT THEIR JOB

To Crowley and Elster, those are the keys to managing up. "If you do those . . . things, you will have a great relationship with your manager," Elster said, laughing. And frankly, I agree. Not everyone will have a supportive manager or even a manager who's capable of understanding the differing levels of privilege the team members have. But part of that shortcoming is because few managers are actually taught how to be managers—and that's not something that can be fixed with management training off-sites, webinars, and motivational speakers. Many of those sessions focus on arbitrary management styles that are difficult to identify in yourself (and even those that make you take tests to try to figure out your own management style are so often out of touch that they're difficult to apply). Crowley explained, "The whole point of managing up and not copping resentment because your boss doesn't know how to manage you, it begins with that assumption. Assume that they don't know really that much of what they're doing."

If you've ever been in a managerial position, think about how much preparation you received for the role. I'm willing to bet you didn't get much of anything, aside from a few pep talks from your own manager. So with the understanding that your manager is probably winging it as much as you are and with the end goal of trying to get along with them, turning them from an adversary to an ally and getting them to recognize and understand how you've been marginalized at work, here are some more tips to make sure you and your manager are always on the same page.

LET YOUR MANAGER KNOW
BEING MARGINALIZED IMPACTS YOUR BEST WORK

First of all, when you tell your manager what's going on, it's important to let them know that what's happening is actually making it more difficult for you to do what you've been hired to do. Don't frame this in terms of your marginalization holding you back or making you less effective at your job, however. Remember when we talked about never letting people see you sweat? That's important for your manager as well. Instead, frame the discussion the other way: You could be doing so much more if you weren't marginalized. You could be doing greater, more impactful things and leading more initiatives and projects. You want your boss to think that if they're happy with your performance now, they should just imagine what you could do if you weren't essentially being ground underfoot by colleagues who want to keep you on the sidelines because they're either jealous, greedy, or just straight-up racist.

Assuming your boss actually cares about you and your well-being at work, you *can* explain that being marginalized is keeping you from talking to the people you need to work with on bigger ideas and projects that could move your entire team forward. Let your boss know that sitting at your desk working on the office housework may keep things moving, but it's also actively preventing you from picking up work that you could excel at. Let them know that you'd like their help in making sure work is assigned more fairly and in keeping an eye out so the loudest person in the room isn't the one making all the decisions on behalf of everyone else.

Ultimately, the bottom line is to communicate to your manager that what you're going through is fixable and you'd like their help figuring out the best way to deal with it. Make them a partner instead of dropping a problem on their desk and walking away. The more collaborative they feel, the more likely they are to lift a finger to help, even if it might make them a little uncomfortable to do so. After all, managers are people too, and on some level, they probably just wish the boat would keep afloat on its own without them having to wade into interpersonal and team dynamics. Besides, would you want to if you were in their shoes?

PROMISE BETTER RESULTS
IF YOUR MANAGER HELPS YOU

Along with letting your manager know that you could be doing even better work than you're already doing if you didn't have to deal with being marginalized at work, go a step further if you're comfortable doing so, and let them know that if they take action, they can expect tangible results. Don't just explain that your being marginalized is keeping you from doing more impactful work; let them know exactly what impact you would have if you were running at your full potential. And let them know that you really want to bring your full potential to the table.

So more specifically, focus on what you can bring to the projects you've been excluded from, and propose what you would do if you were working on those projects. If you've been excluded from meetings where the team shares its big successes for a company newsletter, for example, explain to your boss that if you were invited you'd make a point to include some of the things you know that your team worked on but hasn't gotten recognition for. If you've been left out of a project for which you know you have something to contribute, explain to your boss what, specifically, you could do, and how you would do it, if you were allowed to participate. If you're aware of something that the project is especially lacking, explain how you would make it happen, but don't let it come off as if you're complaining about being marginalized (not that you don't have the right to do that, of course). Letting your manager know there are tangible benefits to assigning you to the projects you've been excluded from—and would like to work on—will give them reasons to make room for you.

LINE UP YOUR PRIORITIES WITH THEIRS

Another way to convince your manager that addressing your concerns, whether they are about assigning work fairly or someone on your team treating you poorly or making you feel unwelcome, is to line up those issues with your boss's priorities. Some of this approach is similar to letting your boss know that you could be doing much more work if the issue were resolved. But it's also worth pointing out the ideas and skills you could bring to the table on some of the other projects and tasks you've been excluded from . . . if only you were allowed to participate.

"I think what you can do is find out how you can make that person look good, with the hope that they would then want to help you look good. But there's no guarantee to that. I think you have a higher chance, though," if you consider your boss's priorities, Elster suggested.

For example, when I learned that I was going to be sidelined on a potential audio project at a previous job, I pointed out to my then manager that I had experience working on podcasts in the past, had edited and produced audio, and even had my own equipment just, you know, in case that kind of information would have been helpful. Sure enough, I wound up on the project. It wasn't the end-all of the issues I had to face there, but at least I was able to claim a seat at the table where there had been none for me before that conversation. Similarly, if you let your manager know that one of your team's priorities is missing out on your expertise and skills, they may be more inclined to assign work fairly in the future in light of what they know. They may take some convincing and may not even know that you have these skills and experience but making sure that they understand you would be an asset to this high-priority project can work out well for you. In the big picture, it's a way to get work assigned fairly, and it gives you opportunities to thrive, which is what you really want. This tactic is especially important if the person who usually gets the glamour work doesn't necessarily deserve it but is just the loudest person in the room, the one who claims credit for everyone's accomplishments but never takes responsibility for the team's failures, much less their own.

This approach has another useful benefit: It allies you with your manager against a problem, not necessarily a person. It proves to your manager that you understand priorities, particularly *their* priorities, and that you want to work on the things that matter the most to the team and, by proxy, the company. I only hope that those priorities are truly what you want to work on, and it's even better if they are, but there's no understating how valuable that allegiance is. It can benefit you if you ever have a big idea you'd like to get started on but you need some help from your manager to get it off the ground. Or you might want to work on a smaller project at some point, a less important one, but something you think you'd be really good at. Your manager may even back you up. Plus, when you align your priorities with your manager's, the manager has the option of injecting you into the spaces you deserve to be, rather than having to force or challenge someone else's behavior. Sidestepping a confrontation with an offending party is a bit of a cop-out, but again, if *you* could avoid a confrontation, wouldn't you if you were in their shoes?

COME ARMED WITH SOLUTIONS

This tip—have solutions ready—is a bit of a double-edged sword, because you also shouldn't wait until you think you have the whole thing sorted out before you talk to your boss. I did that when I felt marginalized and I had a semi-absentee boss. She was receptive to my concerns, but she was already disengaged from our team and focused on her other priorities. I remember telling her once that I didn't want to "complain about something without having some ideas on what we should do to fix it." On the one hand, I think this approach was smart, but on the other hand, it gave her an out to ignore the issues for much longer than it took me to explain them to her. She was sympathetic but did little to address the sense of marginalization I felt beyond encouraging me to spend more time around *her* specifically. Admittedly this advice was quite helpful, although she was so busy I didn't get to take her up on it as often as I would have liked.

That said, having solutions at the ready is really important for people who have managers who won't listen unless they're given something they can act on or managers who don't afford people the psychological safety to discuss concerns. These people know that their bosses will be receptive if they're presented with a fix for the problem. I've had managers who were fun to chat with and super-receptive to my complaints about whatever might be on my mind. But they made it very clear that they wouldn't do anything about anything unless I took time to come up with a potential solution and explained to them exactly what I wanted them to do to fix the problem. Some of them called it "learning to fix my own issues"; others simply wanted to avoid taking responsibility for managing their team. In any case, it helps to come with fixes to your problems if you want faster action—and those fixes probably shouldn't be things like "fire the guy who hates me," as much as you might like them to be.

"I think that kind of boss often feels better if they can give you something," Crowley said. "Think of work-arounds," she suggested. "If you could ask to attend a conference or be on a task force or do a certain project, it's not directly in your line of work but is something that gets you out and more visible but also benefits your boss. That could be one way to work around the marginalized status so that you can gain some visibility." And that's one of the keys—when you're marginalized, you feel isolated and invisible. Finding ways—even work-arounds—that may address that invisibility can help a lot, either in your current job or to gear you up for the next one. "This is about gaining visibility and being able to demonstrate your capabilities one way or another," Crowley said. "If you can't do it in the direct report line, perhaps you can do it outside or interdepartmentally." So for a manager who may be hesitant to deal with marginalization on their teams or to rock the boat and call out bad behavior by other team members, an effort to help you gain visibility gives them a way to boost you without necessarily punishing someone else and to feel like they're doing *something* to address the root problem.

Focus on actionable suggestions for your manager, like, "Hey, I realized that I'm the one who has to book the room and take notes for all our meetings. I recognize that it needs to be done, but it would be great if we could all take turns doing it," when you think you're being saddled with too much of the office housework and you don't have time for the more important things you want to do. You could also try "Hey, I really would love to be in the meetings where we discuss what we're working on with other teams. I haven't been able to get an invite, unfortunately. Could you forward it to me or ask the organizer to include me?" In one breath, you both reiterate the problem you're having and propose a simple, actionable solution that your manager can do to help alleviate the problem.

Don't Fall for Productivity Porn

(PRIORITIZING YOUR WORK)

We're all busy. That's no surprise. We all have our full-time jobs, career prospects, side projects, and responsibilities to family and friends, and the list goes on. Arguably, *busy* is most people's default state. We're all accustomed to being busy.

So, most popular productivity advice is, predictably, aimed at the busy person, the one trying to do more with the same amount of hours in the day that the rest of us have. And sure, that makes sense, but it avoids a very important question: Why are you doing all this work in the first place? And for marginalized people, how can you even try to be truly productive and prioritize if you don't have the kind of work that will advance your career?

See, that's the problem with being just busy. It's easy to confuse the two: being busy and being productive. But being busy means little more than just having a lot to do, and being productive actually implies you're getting those things done in a meaningful way.

Of course, we've all had jobs where our managers couldn't tell the difference, so there's something to be said for looking busy, and I'll address this topic later. But for now, I'm going to assume that you're busy and that you, like me, often turn to productivity advice to try to be *less* busy.

So before you jump on the latest to-do app or project management tool to try to organize your way out of all the things you have to do, step back—or up, as it were. For all its pros and cons, productivity guru and author David Allen's Getting Things Done (GTD) approach to productivity rests on one core principle: that before you spend time doing something, you should examine how it fits into your overall priorities and the rest of the things you have to do. How does this task that you're staring down on your to-do list fit into your goals? Whether it's an email you have to send, a book you have to write, or an event you have to plan, ask yourself why you're doing it. Maybe it's just because your manager asked you to do it and keeping your manager happy will keep you employed and stable, especially for those of us marginalized at work and lacking the power or psychological safety to pick and choose our assignments.

That's fine, to a degree, but even saying yes to everything your manager asks you to do can get you caught up in what's called the *busy trap*, a term popularized by Tim Kreider in an opinion piece in the *New York Times* in 2012.[1] He explained that *busy* has become a kind of persistent state for many of us, where most people meander from task to task in their lives, knowing that after they finish one thing, there's always something else waiting for them to pick up. The busy trap rejects idleness as sloth and laziness and encourages us to always be on the move, always productive, always active and looking for the next thing we have to mark off of our to-do lists. It's so baked into our common consciousness that many of us feel anxious and unsettled when we don't have something to do or when we spend time sleeping or resting instead of working on a side project, hustling to make a side gig profitable, reading more books, or doing more of whatever it is we've convinced ourselves we're not doing enough of.

Kreider rejected this lifestyle wholesale, reminding us that those moments of quiet, idle, do-nothing time are necessary for our emotional and physical health. He also said that it's in those moments of idle contemplation that we're at our most creative and the most open to new hobbies, new passions, and new ideas that may chart the future direction of our lives. He noted that even children succumb to the busy trap, having any semblance of free time drained out of their lives in the quest to stand out in a competitive social and academic world. This trap is even more pronounced for young people of traditionally marginalized backgrounds, who, as mentioned earlier, need to be twice as good as their privileged peers are, to be considered capable in the same areas. If you don't have the money to afford Ivy League tuition, if you're not a legacy family, or if you're an immigrant, a minority, or disabled, you already spend so much time and energy pushing back against systemic discrimination that you need every leg up you can get. So extracurricular activities, intramural sports, and advanced classes all now occupy the time that many school-age children and teenagers used to spend socializing with friends, relaxing, contemplating their futures, and dreaming. This change isn't universally bad, and Kreider didn't characterize it as such (and frankly, neither will I).

Taking the time to expand your horizons is a good thing and

taking the time to advance your knowledge and improve yourself is always something we should aspire to do. But to bring it back around, the key is to remember why you're doing it. Are you taking those language classes because you want to learn the tongue, plan to visit the countries where the language is spoken, or have an interest in the culture and lifestyle of the people who speak it? Or are you taking the classes because you believe you should, to have a good academic or professional résumé? All these reasons can be true, of course, but if you resonate with the latter reason more than the former ones, it might be worth considering doing something else with your all-too-precious time, ideally an activity that both interests you personally and can improve your professional life.

Matching your work with your personal goals is an area where traditional productivity advice tends to fall short. So much of it is focused on helping you do more, but little of the advice encourages you to focus on where your to-dos fit into a bigger picture. And that do-more approach makes some sense. By starting with the assumption that you have a lot to wrangle and it all needs to get done (which is true for many of us), the developers of a to-do app don't have to dissect a complicated question like "Why am I doing all this work, anyway?" That part is up to you. And in a way it should be: Before you add a to-do to your favorite app, you should ask yourself how this fits in with everything else you have to do. For those of us in marginalized groups, you *really* have to ask; otherwise, you'll get caught spinning your wheels on office housework or, worse, busy-work designed to keep you on the sidelines, with no opportunities to grow and improve.

INTERROGATE YOUR WORK

I like to call this next process *interrogating your work,* and the process doesn't always mean you'll escape something you don't want to do, but it does at least mean that in your own head—or even on paper or in that to-do app we're talking about—you can prioritize your work accordingly. For example, if my boss asks me to do something that isn't part of my job, I'm probably going to do it anyway because he asked. Refusing comes with a cost (in terms of career opportunity and favorable standing at work) higher than I'm willing to pay (in terms of time, energy, or, in some cases, money).

The costs of refusal are especially significant for marginalized individuals or groups that are traditionally discriminated against in the workplace. If the toilet in my home bathroom is leaking, I have to call someone to fix it or take time out to fix it myself. There's no getting around those things. But before I tell someone who wants to "pick my brain" that sure, we can hop on a phone call chat and I can offer them advice, I have to think about whether my desire to be helpful is overriding my knowledge that I have only a certain amount of time during the day to get those must-complete tasks done. Interrogating my work helps me make sure I can adequately dedicate the necessary time and energy to the things I have to do. It can prevent me from feeling overwhelmed because I don't have enough time to finish everything or, worse, I only have enough time to do a half-assed job on everything on my list but never enough time to truly excel at any of it. This is another important observation for marginalized folks: We're so often expected to lend our time and energy to help out, be seen as go-getters at work, and then mentor and help others grow and succeed (all of which can be really beneficial, don't get me wrong), that we need to be careful about making sure the time we spend on those things doesn't detract from our own priorities or, worse, our own self-care.

That's the difference between being productive versus being simply busy. And as always, productivity is about finding ways to spend less time on the things you have to do so you can spend more time on the things you want to do.

DON'T FALL FOR THE TRAP OF PRODUCTIVITY FOR THE SAKE OF PRODUCTIVITY

Beyond interrogating your work, the next step is to understand and resist the draw to all things productivity. Ideally, you find something that works for you, or something that you can massage into a method that works for you, and then apply said method and get to work. You'd only spend time looking into new methods and new tools if something comes up that addresses a need you have or fixes a problem you've been working around or struggling with. To do anything more runs the risk of obsession, which Vivek Haldar, former Google developer, calls *productivity porn*. When you are seduced by productivity porn, you spend so much time obsessing over new and interesting productivity tips, methods, and tools that you either don't have the time to apply any of them to your actual work or you don't bother actually working, instead choosing to pretend you're being productive by obsessing about productivity. If you've ever spent time procrastinating by organizing your to-do list instead of actually doing the things on that list, you know what I mean. I asked Haldar about the origin of the concept of productivity porn, and he pointed me to an article by Matt Heinz, published in 2012 in the tech blog *GeekWire*. In the piece, Heinz explained that his wife had come to call his obsession with productivity reading "productivity porn."[2] Heinz promised that in future columns, he would cut through the advice and only offer the most useful tidbits.

I also experienced as a project manager lots of discussion about the *quantified self*, a concept suggesting that if you kept track of every quantifiable detail of your life, you could apply data analysis to it to determine, for example, the best time to have lunch. "That 2000s culture eventually morphed into the hustle culture of the late 2010s, which by now feels utterly hollow and meaningless," Haldar told me, and I agree. We're seeing the results of it in today's gig economy, where all of us are encouraged to keep moving and keep working, regardless of our personal needs or desires, and which is conveniently forcing us to do so simply to survive.

PRODUCTIVITY PORN IS AIMED AT THOSE WITH PRIVILEGE

Haldar also sees much of today's productivity porn as truly only useful to the people with the privilege to leverage it. For example, David Allen and Seth Godin, both incredible authors and speakers who became popular in the 2000s, generally aim their advice at white-collar workers, who have the creative freedom and time to tweak their workflows to find an optimal balance. "I do see a lot of productivity advice coming from folks who are already in a comfortable position and presuming the luxury of having a lot of time (to build and tweak your system), money (to get all that cool gear), and sanity," Haldar explained. "If you're low on Maslow's hierarchy, you're not thinking of fine-tuning your project setups. A C-level executive often has the luxury of clearing out their calendar for a week to 'reset' and regain their focus and priorities, something that a junior- to mid-level employee obviously doesn't."[3] He continued, "The rest of the productivity-industrial complex really turned me off and came off as sleazy and preying on the hopes and dreams of young, early-career people by serving up the dream of a magic potion that would unleash their productivity and make them successful in life."

TAKE WHAT YOU NEED, LEAVE THE REST

For me, Haldar's perspective also rings true, but having seen how peers in the same organization (people with similar jobs but different backgrounds) have different luck applying the same productivity techniques at the same jobs, I learned a few lessons. There's a little bit more at play than just class and seniority, and while you can certainly learn things from the so-called productivity industry, you should take what you can use and leave the rest behind—and then focus on doing what you do best.

It might sound ironic, a book about productivity telling you to stop reading so much about productivity, but my message here should be clear: When you find something that works for you, put it into practice and spend less time refining your methods and more time actually getting the work done. If your method proves to be an obstacle to achieving your goals, then revisit the method. If there are pain points in your method—and there will undoubtedly be—then take aim at them. But your method should be a conduit to getting things done, not another task for you to take on.

Haldar explained, "My motivation for juxtaposing *productivity* with *porn* was that, just like porn, [productivity] is something seductive and titillating but ultimately meaningless and hollowing. It's an addiction that you can shovel endless amounts of time and effort into. It doesn't serve you." When I asked him if he thought people had moved past the treadmill of productivity tips or were collectively still on it, he was clear: "It's more relevant now than ever. The industry and marketing around productivity have only grown since then (just look at all the productivity gurus on YouTube). There are more gadgets, notebooks, journals, and courses being sold around the topic than ever before. And the term *porn* is even more apt, as people fetishize the perfect apps (and color themes!) and gear (the perfect desk setup!)." I feel a little guilty because there was definitely a time when I contributed to that discourse, sharing photographs of people's carefully customized desktops and workspaces. And to be completely honest, I still enjoy looking at desk setups, lighting, keyboards, and mouse mats all customized just so. But on the bright side, I recognize these things for what they are: elements of personalization and customization that can help you feel more at home at a workspace, not elements required to boost your productivity. They're like looking at a design catalog for inspiration: It's fun, but it doesn't actually do the work of redecorating or renovating your home.

This advice is especially important for people of marginalized groups or folks who are underrepresented in the workplace. After all, it's easy to say that you should just not do things that aren't aligned with your personal or professional goals, but it's another to figure out a way to avoid those to-dos when they're dropped on your desk, so to speak.

Try to remember your own limits, and before you say yes to another project, interrogate it and determine whether you truly have the time, energy, and mental space to do the project justice and bring your full vision to it. If you don't think you can do it the way you'd really want it done, say no. If you don't have the option, such as when your boss brings work to your desk and demands that you take care of it, you may not have a choice. But you do have the choice to either accept it quietly or ask for more information or resources to help you do the best work you can. If you know that this new project is just going to add to an already-full plate, bring that up with your manager (as we discussed in Rule 7, about managing up), and ask if something else on your to-do list can go on the back burner while you focus on this new item. Ask how important the new assignment is and how you should prioritize it, given all of the other things you have going on. Explain that you don't want to mess this new assignment up, but you have a lot going on and you want to make sure you do the best job possible.

Once you get the hang of interrogating your work, it's a powerful tool to help you make sure that you understand exactly what you're working on and how much time and attention you can give to any one task. It makes sure you're actively engaged with your work, as opposed to its being a waterfall you passively stand under and then ask yourself, "Why am I so wet?" Interrogating your work will also help you make time for the other things that you enjoy, whether they are the side projects you've been meaning to hustle on or just taking time out for the important things in life, like family or friends or a good book. However, some people have more difficulty than others do to get to this point or to say no in the workplace at all. So before you turn to productivity apps and other tools to some-how unlock your full potential, keep in mind that many of those tools are made *by* people with privilege and *for* people with similar privilege. In the next rule, however, we'll look at how some of these products and approaches can be modified to work for marginalized people.

RULE 9

Give Your In-Box Its Time, but No More

(BEING MINDFUL)

T he always-connected nature of our twenty-first-century workplace may seem to only offer disadvantages to those without privilege. But while there's absolutely no doubt the modern workplace is designed to erode the boundaries you place between your work and the rest of your life and that the osmosis works both ways, here are a few tips to help you take control of your work life.

First, just because everyone is online all the time doesn't mean you have to pay attention to every single notification you get. Or rather, it may mean you have to take note of it but not pay attention to it. You probably receive your work email on your smartphone. In fact, so many of us do that in some workplaces, this easy access is more of a drawback than an optional way to stay in touch with a boss who may need a way to get in touch with you after hours or in case of emergencies. Think for a moment about how quickly business communication has changed: how quickly we've gone from workplaces where email wasn't really a thing to workplaces where we're all expected to have Slack and Gmail installed on our devices, connected to our work accounts and always ready to see and respond to notifications, even if it's technically "okay" if we don't respond right away. It's a bit insidious, but that training set in fast, didn't it? The transformation happened in a matter of a few years. And for those of us who are marginalized at work and are expected to jump at the office housework and keep the team running smoothly no matter what time it may be and whether we're in the office or out today, it's even more important to learn to disassociate the ping of a new email with the stress of having to do something about it.

So here are a few suggestions based on my years of being always on and stressed out about it, and years more of being always on and *not* stressed about it at all: Schedule your notifications, and then schedule your email sessions. Most email apps and services, by default, want to push you a notification as soon as a new message hits your in-box, whenever that may be. Instead, set your email app to only check for email every set number of minutes. This is usually an option you can find in the app's settings or in your web browser. I recommend every fifteen to thirty minutes during a workday and then only every hour during off-hours in case of emergencies, if you have to check during your off time at all. That way, you still get informed about important things but just on a more manageable timetable that won't interfere with anything else you may be working on during the day or with your own private life during the evening.

Similarly, I also suggest blocking out time during your workday specifically to managing your in-box. It can be tempting to try to sort out all your emails the first thing in the morning or the last thing before you go to bed. Or worse, you might think that you'll give yourself a head start on the next day by staying up until midnight when you have to be up at six the next morning. Or you might ruin your Sunday by spending the last precious hours of the weekend in hopes of an easier Monday morning. Now if you're a morning person or your workload is the lightest in the morning, then book yourself an hour or so in the morning dedicated to email time.

When I was a project manager, I found that most people left the office around 5 or 6 p.m., but I enjoyed working late because I could put on my headphones and listen to music, and I didn't have a long commute home. So I made sure to book the late hours of the workday, usually between 5 and 7 o'clock, as my email time. Some days, I needed the whole time. Other times, I only needed a few minutes and I left early. Either way, the time was productive. Sure, I used the time to manage my email, but I also always knew that this time was on my calendar. The set schedule diffused the stress of getting messages during the day and wondering when I would have time to read or reply to them. I could even glance at messages just to stay aware of what was going on, without feeling the pull to jump into a conversation or reply right away, because I knew that time to do just that was on the calendar. If an issue was important, if I needed to jump into a conversation to appear engaged, I could always drop what I was doing and switch focus. But if I didn't have to, I wouldn't, because my in-box had a dedicated time when I would focus on it. It didn't need more.

But don't forget that latter part—about making sure not to miss an urgent matter—okay? A more privileged person could stop here and just ignore their in-box except for scheduled times. Those of us without those same privileges have to be more careful. The freedom to not reply to every little thing means you have to be sure to reply to the important things so that you're always engaged, you're always aware and watching, and, of course, you always look busy.

CHOOSE WHEN TO REPLY TO CERTAIN MESSAGES, AND SCHEDULE YOUR REPLIES

Once you manage the influx of emails, it's time to do something about the outflow. As I just mentioned, being acutely aware of what's coming in and being able to judge what needs your attention *right now* versus later in the day is only part of the issue. The other part is making sure that you know when and how to respond to the right conversations.

For example, you'll want to jump in to reply to something that demands your attention (or to avoid missing an opportunity for glamour work before you-know-who replies to snag it). You'll want to reply to your boss if they're asking if you're free for a meeting this afternoon. You don't need to reply if your boss is asking for a report that they won't look at until Monday. You don't need to reply if someone is just posting an update in an ongoing thread that's been batting back and forth all day. You don't need to reply if someone is just checking in or wants time to pick your brain.

If the email is after-hours, you probably don't need to reply at all, unless you know that doing so will either earn you a ton of brownie points at work or that whoever sent it will want the answer sooner rather than later. The same goes for texts, even more so. Texting is a great way to get ahold of someone in a pinch or an emergency but try to protect your boundaries whenever possible. Keep your replies short and aimed at shifting the conversation to something else if you can. As we move to an always-on, always-available way of work, it's no surprise our managers want our phone numbers to text and communicate for routine issues, not just emergencies. If you're comfortable working that way, great. Just make sure you don't get sucked into responding to a text from your boss at 11 p.m. the way you would from a friend—because your boss, and your employer, isn't your friend. Look, reply and acknowledge the text if you're worried they'll be mad you left them unread, and get back to them in the morning.

I've had people who email at 9 p.m. and want to meet the following morning. In some of those cases, I'd need to jump on a response immediately and schedule the meeting. In other cases, I'd get an email from my boss, who would say, "Hey, you don't need to get back to me until morning," and I'd do it anyway just to get the win.

So for those important messages, you know the drill. Shift focus, try to get it done quickly, and then try to shift back to whatever you're working on. Try not to let the interruption totally disrupt your focus and try not to get caught up in other things that may be lurking in your in-box at the same time. Remind yourself that there will be a time for that, and it's already there on your calendar. For the less important messages but those that will earn you points, you have two more options. You can either reply right away, even if you're awake at 3 a.m. and want to run the risk of the follow-up in the morning: "Wow, you were up at three a.m.?" Or you can schedule the reply to go out at a more reasonable hour so that you look like you're awake and active early, even if you're not. Of course, that tactic could fall apart if the recipient tries to follow up with you through another channel or replies right away to a message you scheduled for 6 a.m., but that's still you clearly being responsive and proactive.

In the newsroom, I worked frequently with journalists who lived all over the globe. I learned quickly that it was just as helpful for me to schedule my emails so they arrived at a decent time of day for them as it was for my colleagues to do the same. I wound up taking that approach with everyone—managers, potential projects, meeting requests, you name it. Instead of sending a message out at the end of my workday, or over lunch even, I would schedule that message to go out at the beginning of the following day, so I would be around and free to discuss or answer follow-up questions if there were any. For a while it felt like I should have just gotten it over with immediately but remember: There's always going to be more email, more work, more follow-ups, more messages. If you can buy yourself even a good night's sleep by scheduling something to go out in the morning rather than right away, do it. You're still getting the job done and knocking something off your to-do list, and you're taking care of yourself in the process.

And speaking of taking care of yourself, here's the trouble with being known as the colleague who never sleeps or who always seems to reply to emails at 3 a.m. Getting that reputation at a job may mean you're valued and you're passionate and engaged, but it comes at the cost of your own life. So take it from someone who has frequently been that person—if you do it, just make sure you do just enough to earn the rep, but not so often that you're actually *not sleeping*. Remember, we're trying to look busy, not be so busy we drive ourselves into an early grave.

FIND YOUR PRODUCTIVE HOURS

Are you a morning person or a night person? Don't worry, no judgment here. I'm not a morning person at all. I try to start my days as late as possible, and I don't mind working even later into the evening. I don't really *feel* awake and productive until . . . well . . . what a lot of people consider lunchtime. For example, when I worked in a more traditional office, we were generally expected to adhere to an 8 to 9 a.m. start time, and people used to take lunch around 11:30 a.m. or noon. For me, I barely feel awake and aware of my surroundings by 11:30 a.m. Sure, I'd drag myself out of bed to get to the office at 8 a.m. if I had to, but I hated it, every time. But part of that is because those just aren't my most productive hours of the day. So think back to the last time you were really in the zone—what time of day was it? Do you find yourself more likely to get into the zone or to be more productive at a certain time of the day? Maybe the late afternoons or even in the early evenings? Maybe you're truly a morning person and you love the quiet of the mornings before other people wake up or are at least awake enough to bother you. Maybe you, like me, sometimes have your most productive hours in the middle of the night, when the rest of the world is asleep.

Obviously, you can't get too much work done if your productive hours are the middle of the night and your boss expects you in your seat at 8 a.m., or schedules you for morning meetings at 9 a.m., but you can work around it. Schedule your lowest-lift tasks—your in-box time, reading through and updating documents, looking over proposals, or whatever else may (ostensibly) be the most brainless part of your workday—for when you know you aren't really awake or present enough to do your best work. You know, the stuff you'd probably phone in anyway. Personally, I use the mornings—if I have to be awake at all—for things like emptying my in-box, replying to easily handled messages, and updating spreadsheets with the activities for the day (or the next day, even). Then that way, when I feel the most productive—usually in the afternoons and evenings—I try to keep my calendar clear (but blocked off, if need be) so that I can dive into the things I need to do without distractions. For me, it's anything that requires interaction with other people, like meetings, writing, or editing other people's writing—anything that demands some level of focus and deep work.

See how flexible your calendar is so that you can make sure that the times you know you're the most productive are when you do the things that really matter.[1] If you wind up doing the least meaningful work during your best hours, you're wasting your energy and your potential. That's the time you should be spending on the biggest projects: the glamour assignment that you managed to get or, barring any of that, your pet projects or secret side hustle that's going to get you out of the bad spot you're in and into something much better. Obviously scheduling your most important tasks for your optimum times is hard to do if, for example, you work best in the middle of the night, because you need to sleep so that you can go to work in the morning. So don't go that far. But maybe you're a morning person and you seldom get to spend the mornings working on the things you wish you could. You wind up struggling because the after-lunch sleepies hit and you have to get through leading meetings while you're falling asleep. Your colleagues may hate it, but it sounds like you need to book those meetings first thing in the morning, when you're the most energetic. (Just be aware that some of your coworkers, like me, will probably be nursing their coffees and feeling half dead. We appreciate bagels or doughnuts, though.)

WORK IN BURSTS, NOT CONSTANTLY (TAKE BREAKS!)

This advice may be a little counterintuitive, but if there's one thing that I learned in my years working at *Lifehacker*, it's that a wealth of research points out that the harder you work, the worse you are at whatever it is you're doing. Instead, the key to better productivity is to take breaks between working sessions.[2] What's that, you say? Work *less* to do *more*? Well, think about it: Or rather, think about the last time you slaved away at something for hours on end. By the end of it, how did you feel? If you finished, you probably felt accomplished, but you were most likely drained, tired, and ready for a break. Now imagine that you *didn't* finish, so that sense of accomplishment wouldn't have been there. Maybe you worked for hours on something you knew you'd have to pick up again tomorrow. You probably felt tired and stressed and needed to stop in order to start fresh the next morning or the next time you picked it up. Now think about how you feel when you settle down to start working: You're probably more energetic and engaged, even if you were reluctant to get started. You were in more of a headspace to let yourself get into the zone, and you had the energy to get into it.

So the key to using breaks to boost your productivity is to leverage the rule of working in bursts and taking breaks. Before you get bogged down and feel run down by your work, give yourself a break and a chance to recharge. Switch to another task, or if you prefer (and I certainly prefer), get up and stretch, take a walk around your office or your block, make yourself a cup of tea (or whatever you prefer to drink; just remember you're trying to work here), and then come back after a few minutes and jump in again. The goal is to give yourself some recovery time between heavy work sessions so that your brain can reset and your physical stress symptoms can subside a bit. It really helps. You may feel as if you need to always be at your desk to be viewed as dependable. But getting up and moving around will make you fresher and clearer-headed. Many managers assume that if you're not at your desk, butt firmly in seat, you can't possibly be productive, but the idea of high productivity by working all the time is inherently flawed. You do your best work when you're not fatigued. Your boss *should* want you to take breaks to refresh yourself and come back energized, but too many managers just assume that if you're at your desk, you're working. So try to take your breaks when you can and incorporate them into your work style.

In fact, a number of popular productivity methods are based on a work-then-rest pattern, and more and more research has indicated that if you keep up this pattern, you'll get more done, depending on the kind of work you do. For example, the *pomodoro technique*, invented in the early 1990s by developer and author Francesco Cirillo, uses an on-off system in which you work deeply and focus on one task for a short period and then take a break. With Cirillo's approach, you take large batches of work, break them down into specific tasks that you can focus on, and then set about working on one task for twenty-five minutes. Cirillo even used an actual tomato-shaped desk timer to keep track of the time (thus the name *pomodoro*), so you would know to stop working when the timer went off. When it did go off, you'd mark down a check on a piece of paper or some other thing you'd use to keep track of how many twenty-five-minute sessions you had worked. Then, you'd take a break for a few minutes. Cirillo suggested five, but you could make it even as long as ten if you need to. Get up, stretch, refill your water bottle (stay hydrated!), grab a quick snack. Then you reset the timer and go back to it for another twenty-five minutes and repeat the process. After every four checkmarks (each of these work-and-break sessions is also, confusingly, often referred to as a pomodoro), you take a longer break, like fifteen to thirty minutes or however long it takes for you to feel refreshed and ready to start the whole process over again.

The method has been remarkably popular with developers and creatives, who have large amounts of work that they need to focus on for long periods. It often works for me because I have writing or editing projects to work on, so I can set a timer, go heads-down for a while, and then come up for air and a break to reset my mind. Not everyone has the privilege of working this way, of course, but this is really just a scaffold—a way to structure your work so you don't drain yourself too quickly. You use short breaks to recharge and regroup mentally before you dive back in and get more stuff done. In many ways, despite the number of breaks you may feel you're taking, you're getting more done in those deep work sessions than you probably think, and you'll feel better at the end of the day, to boot.

I spoke with David Kadavy, author of one of my favorite books, *The Heart to Start: Stop Procrastinating and Start Creating*, and his most recent book, *Mind Management, Not Time Management*, has a lot to say about the importance of saving your mental energy for the important work. Once you've saved that energy, he told me, "the second prong of the strategy is to make better use of that energy in the event you are entrusted with a glamour project. To shine on a glamour project, you need to think creatively, and you can multiply the impact of each precious moment you get."

This is another way that taking breaks is remarkably powerful. "Take advantage of the power of incubation," Kadavy said. "When you think about a problem, then step away from it, your mind works on the problem in the interim. Popular wisdom says we should sleep on it when we face a tough problem, and we've all experienced the clarity of returning to a problem after a break. But few of us use this 'passive genius' intentionally." So if you work really deeply and then spend your break times dreaming or thinking about how you can make your pet projects work or your personal goals achievable, there's a reason why.

"In between grunt-work tasks," Kadavy said, "take just a moment to brainstorm something on a glamour project. It could be two minutes of typing a bullet-point list of thoughts. You have to overcome any perfectionist tendencies to do this, so throw away all expectations of quality in these short sessions. (Don't let your colleagues see this rough work!) When you get another moment between tasks, return to your notes—better yet, start again from scratch."

This tip is related to one of my favorite productivity tips that's applicable to work, life, or anything else: *Just get started*. For marginalized workers, progress can feel insurmountable. If you are dreaming of something, working toward a goal, or, as Kadavy mentioned earlier, in between breaks and brainstorming, then spending even a few minutes to get your thoughts or ideas into some kind of motion—whether it's notes, a drawing, or something else tangible— is often enough to make a difference. Even if you tell yourself,

"I'll work on it for just five minutes," those five could easily turn to ten or fifteen if you hit your stride, and even if you have to go back to work after thirty or stop after fifteen, you have something to show for yourself.

"You'll be amazed how much clearer your thoughts are after a short brainstorm and returning to the problem from another task," Kadavy told me. "While you were doing something else, your brain was working on the problem, subconsciously. The effects are even more pronounced if you get a night's sleep between sessions. This is why, before bed every night, playwright Lillian Hellman read aloud dialogue she was working on. She then revisited it in the morning."

THE SURPRISING UPSIDE OF BEING MARGINALIZED

Now here's the broader catch, though: To be able to set aside time to work deeply on the things that matter without distraction or interruption, you'll either need to remove yourself from distractions or come to some kind of agreement with your colleagues that you shouldn't be bothered while you're trying to focus. That's something not all workers can do. If you're forced to do all the housework in an office, it can be difficult or even impossible to find the time. But if your marginalization means you're left out of things, then it might be easier than you think. At the *Times*, I often went entire weeks without seriously engaging with anyone else in the office unless I chose to or forced my presence on someone else. Organizationally, the paper was (and, in many ways, I was also) content to let me just keep working, no meetings or second opinions required. So the upside of being marginalized was that I could focus on deep work when I wanted to. I didn't need to worry about people coming up to my desk and interrupting me. Now, when I was a project manager and was relied on more heavily, I was not marginalized at that job; to the contrary, I was rather empowered. For this reason, I had to take measures to block off time for intensive work and even grab my laptop and charger, find a quiet corner or unused conference room somewhere in the building, and really get down to business.

Whatever works best for you, go for it. Just keep in mind that as word gets out that you're actually being productive, those same folks who wouldn't look at your calendar before scheduling you may also stop respecting those time blocks you set aside for deep work. You might have to get creative to preserve your best hours for the work that matters. Either way, make sure you take those breaks—I found that the breaks between these concentrated work sessions weren't just good for making sure I was hydrated and had a chance to stretch my legs. They also gave me the chance to make sure I didn't miss an email I needed to answer or to get up and walk around the floor and say hello to that colleague I'd been meaning to catch up with. Other times, though, it was enough to stop working and watch some adorable animal videos on YouTube— whatever helps you relax and gets you back in the headspace to start fresh when the break is over.

NEVER LET THEM SEE YOU SWEAT
(IT'S ALWAYS UNDER CONTROL)

Finally, and perhaps most important, *keep your cool*. Remember that regardless of other people's interpretation of your work, you have it under control. Even if you don't feel like you do, don't let other people perceive that you've lost the plot. Being honest and open with your manager is one thing, but with your peers—especially those who go to lengths to exclude you and keep you marginalized? They don't need to know when you're struggling, and they don't need to see you as anything more than capable, confident, and assertive.

This is another place where you can use the always-on nature of the modern workplace to your benefit. If you're marginalized because of ethnicity, background, disability, or even gender or sexuality, all those things come with assumptions on the part of others. They may think that for whatever reason, you're less engaged with your work or less likely to react coolly or objectively to events in the office. Your goal now is to try to be cordial but unaffected, and email and chat are the best places to do this. When everyone else is flying off the handle in a heated email thread about some project that's gone off the rails, you have the opportunity to jump in as the voice of reason, calmly stating the facts and outlining what needs to be done to resolve the issue. That's just an example (and you have to be careful that chiming in as the voice of reason doesn't always mean that you wound up assigning yourself the work that needs to be done). But even appearing to have everything under control goes a long way toward making sure other people think you have everything under control and thus work well under pressure.

After all, many of us who are already discriminated against in majority-white or majority-male workplaces—women and people of color, specifically—have unearned social reputations for being aggressive, overly emotional, or difficult to work with. These perceptions reflect subconscious fears that wind up materializing in the minds of our colleagues whenever they have to work with us on an issue that may be tense or difficult. It's awful to have to say this, but it's on us to rein in our emotions and be unaffected (but remember, stay cordial, because the other side of the coin is that you're too cold, unapproachable, or not a team player!) rather than on our colleagues to address their prejudices. But until our colleagues are forced to deal with their subconscious prejudices the way we're forced to consciously adapt our behavior to them, it's sadly on us to pave a better path for ourselves. For now, at least.

IMPRESSION MANAGEMENT

I spoke with Adam Grant about this concept of control over your workload, and he said that it sounded similar to the idea of impression management, which is definitely the subject of a body of research. "I think one of the more surprising findings, and this is true not only in job interviews but also looking at people's performance evaluations on the job, is that, in general, ingratiation tends to work better than self-promotion," he explained. "In other words, instead of going around and trying to tell everyone about the amazing work you've done, you want your boss to know that you have a high opinion of them.

"It's a self-protective mechanism, and I think the reason that it tends to work is, actually, it's not about you. I'm sure you know the research on this too, but I'm just thinking this is another example of where we have the gender data. I'm afraid that the race data are the same or worse, but I don't know them to the same degree. I don't think they've been studied rigorously or systematically yet. Women just get killed for self-promotion. It's a violation of the norm of humility and modesty, and men get away with it. Men who self-promote are seen sometimes as more competent, and there's no cost to being [a self-promoter]. Whereas women who self-promote sometimes get the competence bonus. Other times, it doesn't work for them, and then they're seen as bitchy, basically. I suspect there are some similar land mines for people of color.

"I think the risk is that you get perceived as self-serving. The Dave Hekman and Stefanie Johnson work shares that you have to be really careful about advocating for diversity if you come from a diverse background, because you're seen as nepotistic and trying to advance your own group. If you're perceived as self-promoting, there's a similar risk and that's where I think ingratiation, the flattery of the people above you, the ability to make them feel and look good is actually in some ways as important politically in an organization as it is to look like you're busy on your work."[3]

Create the Productivity System That Works for You

(DOING THE WORK)

Okay, it's finally time to talk Productivity with a capital *P*— the actual act of getting things done so you can focus your time and energy on what you truly want to do.

That means the things that matter most *to you*. It might be a pet project, a side hustle, a business you want to build, a certification you want to get, or—more idly and honestly—just spending more time with your family, being there for your friends, playing an instrument, or anything else that you find personally rewarding. A problem I've perpetually had with the concept of productivity, ever since my *Lifehacker* days, is this: Even the word *productivity* has been co-opted by people who want to help you do more and more with less time, people who are eager to sell you tips so you can more fully throw yourself into the gaping maw of the corporate beast, to dash yourself on the grinding teeth of the gears of the workplace. They're happy to sell you books on the topic, especially the ones they wrote themselves. They're happy to sell you apps and services aimed at encouraging you to do more; they will set up timers to help you stay on task, offer names for the folders you should keep in your email, or suggest ways you should organize your in-box. Plus, virtually all of them ignore a sobering truth for us members of marginalized groups: Before you can spend time prioritizing your work and figuring out what you should spend time on and what you should put aside, you need to have assignments valuable enough to organize in the first place. You need the right work—and none of those productivity gurus discuss how to get that or even what that looks like, the way I've outlined glamour work and housework, for example.

All of those techniques on their own may not necessarily be harmful, but embracing them without understanding *why* you're embracing them or what you hope to accomplish is like jumping into a Formula One race car and thinking, "I have a driver's license. I can just take it slow and figure this out while I drive." Trust me: You won't.

THE BENEFITS OF DEEP THOUGHTS

One of the people I wanted to talk to about productivity tips, and specifically about how these tips have evolved over time, was my friend and former *New York Times* colleague (now at the *New Yorker* and author of books like *Smarter Faster Better* and *The Power of Habit*) Charles Duhigg. "The ability to identify what the right question is and then make the right decision—that pays enormous dividends," Duhigg explained to me. "The question is, how do you arrange your life in such a way that you have the space and the mental habits to engage in a process where you make better decisions? Not only because you're making the right decision, but also because you're seeing the right problem. It's not like this is particularly new. Peter Drucker said, 'There is nothing more unproductive than finding the optimal solution to the wrong question.'"

Duhigg said that part of the core message he wanted to communicate with *Smarter Faster Better* was that the focus—especially in the early 2010s' start-up and hustle culture—on finding the right productivity technique was a bit misplaced. "Ultimately," he said, "what the research shows is that thinking more deeply has always been the killer productivity app."

So let's step back a moment. I encourage you, before you even think about how you can be more productive and which productivity system you should embrace, *to think good and long about what actually matters to you.* More than likely, performing well at your job is high on that list; otherwise, you wouldn't be here. That's fine, but what else? What aspects of your work do you find personally fulfilling? Which parts make you feel the most accomplished when you leave your workplace every day? What if, and it's definitely *if,* you could only do that work, and nothing else? What would have to happen to make that a reality? (Note: I get it, we all have things about our jobs that we don't like. I'm not trying to say you'll ever get there, but this exercise will help you identify what matters most to you, personally, at work, and what doesn't. That's a different process than figuring out what matters to your *team* or your *manager.*)

Great. Now stop thinking about work and think about the rest of your life. What else matters to you? Maybe you're an avid video gamer and you have a group of friends who you play with and playing with them makes you happy. That's great! Factor that in here. Maybe you're a bit of a social butterfly and love going to bars with your friends on the weekends. Awesome. Make sure you note that you need this friend time to feel recharged and ready for everything else life throws at you. Maybe you have a child who's getting older and thinking about joining a sports team—that means you get to see your little one play team-based games and you really want to be there for them. Or maybe they're going to drama camp and someone needs to go see those plays, and you can't wait to sign up. Perfect, note that desire, too. All of those things take time, and we all only have twenty-four hours in a day.

REMIX OTHER PRODUCTIVITY METHODS TO MEET YOUR NEEDS

Here's another place I'm going to depart from a bunch of traditional productivity advice. Often you'll hear people say (and I've been guilty of saying this in the past myself), "This wealthy person or that successful actor or businessperson has the same twenty-four hours that you do, and they manage to get so much more done, so what's stopping you?" Reject this notion out of hand.

When I spoke to Vivek Haldar about productivity porn and the litany of productivity systems and organizational tools to choose from, he explained something that has matched my personal and professional experience: "To me the ultimate kicker was that *not one* of the role models around me had anything like an explicitly designed 'productivity system.' They all had homegrown systems held together by spit and glue, cobbling together notes, calendars, email, task reminders, et cetera. People would look at me funny if I asked them what was in their 'tickler folder.' What they did have was a ton of time spent deeply engaging with a problem or domain and building expertise and relationships." In short, there's nothing wrong with remixing.

So unless you too—like the C-level executive or the serial

entrepreneur—have the budget to pay for people to do all the little things that add up to many hours in a day, from cleaning your house to cooking meals, seeing the kids off to school, doing the laundry, booking your appointments, checking your email, and so on, the argument is false. The rest of us out here have to make the most of the time we have while still fitting in the stuff we both want and don't want to do. And speaking of the things you don't want to do or the things that have to get done, no matter what, make note of those as well.

Duhigg agreed. He spoke of what has only recently become more evident for him: "The right thing to do is to basically say, 'How ought I prioritize my time?' and then once you've come up with a priority is, 'How do I just make sure that I execute on them?'" So instead of focusing first on which technique works for people like you or people who work in the same field you do, think instead about what you're trying to organize, and why.

"I think that that process should always be changing," Duhigg said. "If pomodoro works for you for a little while, that's great and you learn something from it. Then you find that you don't need it, and so you fill your calendar with what you're going to do that day. There's no one tactic that is the right tactic. It's a mindset that everything I do should be to avoid distractions from anything that is not essential and that makes it harder for me to think more deeply about what I'm doing right now."

MAKE TWO LISTS

Ideally you should have two lists: One list represents the things you love doing. These things bring you joy, happiness, rest and recuperation, or personal fulfillment either at work or while doing the passion work that you choose to do even if you're not necessarily paid for it. The second list represents the things you don't necessarily want to do, but they need doing, no matter how you feel about them. And don't get me wrong, I'm not saying that "vacuum the floors every week" can't be fun if you enjoy vacuuming (I actually do), but it belongs on the must-do list, not the love-it list.

Now put your love-it list aside and focus on the must-do list. *This* is the list for which you're going to apply every productivity hack, trick, and technique that works for you. For the items on this list, you'll want to use every trick in the book to whittle down the amount of time you spend on them (without sacrificing quality, of course!). Let's tackle this list first, applying the following four steps to each item on the list.

1. DO YOU REALLY HAVE TO DO THIS?

By this question, I mean, does this task have to be done at all? Very often we get stuck in situations where we *feel* as if we have to do something that we could opt out of, if we only had either the courage to say no or the opportunity to. Maybe it's worth making the opportunity to push that task off your plate if you can, even if it's difficult to do so. If doing so will pay dividends in time that you could then put to that other list—the things that actually bring you joy—then it's probably worth trying to take this task off your plate. Alternatively, maybe it's something that simply doesn't need to be done at all, if you're willing to part with the task on a personal level. Maybe at work, you're the one who always orders because you have a dietary requirement and don't want to trouble anyone else with it.

Ask yourself, "Would the time I get back from not having to do this multiple times a week be more or less valuable than the awkwardness of asking my boss to round-robin the chore or asking my colleague to take it over?"

Duhigg explained that in some cases, we get so caught up in organizing and doing work that doesn't have to be done at all that it impacts everything we actually want to spend our time on. Everyone differs on what that important work is and what conditions determine their need to achieve it. "For me," he said, "the thing that makes me most productive is having an empty calendar. Again, the goal isn't to have an empty calendar." He explained the difference between what the opportunity for productivity looks like and the act of being productive. He doesn't spend his time taking meetings in order to keep his calendar *full*; he makes sure his calendar is *empty* so that he can do other things.

"The thing is that a full calendar is a leading indicator that I'm not making the right decisions," Duhigg said. "If I look at a calendar and it's got four things for the week, then I know that I have plenty of time to report and write. Then number two is, I just don't do a lot of emails. Sometimes, I'll just look and I'll see how many emails have I sent today. I've probably sent, two, four, six, eight, I've sent nine emails. Three of those were to you." He was referring to our interview. He continued, "There used to be days when I would try and get to in-box zero. I'd see I sent forty-five emails today or fifty emails. I thought that was a productive day. I think that that was exactly wrong. I was the exact opposite of productive. Now, I just basically let them all build up, and then every so often, I'll go through and I'll just hit Delete and shoot off some three-word responses, but that's what works for me."

Now before you take this discussion as the perfect excuse to just leave your in-box alone forever and forget about email and to say that I told you that in-box zero was a scam, Duhigg came to this conclusion because he understood that what he wanted to do—and what his employers were paying him to do—was not to manage a clean in-box. That wasn't his job. His job was to report and to write. And if keeping a clean in-box helps you do that, then fine, but it wasn't helping him. It was a distraction. "I think that there are other people who, for instance, like if you're managing people, then sending a lot of emails is a signal that you're doing things correctly," he said.

2. CAN SOMEONE ELSE DO IT?

A lot of productivity gurus will frame this question as a matter of delegating. And on some level, it is, but this tactic is less about finding someone else to do the work for you and for you to supervise (a very white-collar, office-work approach to everything); maybe the work is something that you don't have to do at all. This consideration is especially important for marginalized people who wind up getting the work that no one else on the team wants or the office housework. We often wind up in positions where we think we can't offload tasks to others, but in reality, help is sometimes just a question away. So is a better working relationship with someone on your team or in your company, if you're willing to work with them the way you'd like to be worked with.

My old boss, Adam Pash, an incredible editor and an even better person, wrote an excellent piece for *Lifehacker* back when I was still a staff writer there. He explained that "if money can buy happiness, spend it." In short, if you have the money to make a problem go away, that money is well spent, even if you don't think throwing money at the problem would be a good idea. In Pash's case, he and his wife had drastically different ideas of what a well-kept house looked like, and the difference was causing tension between them. One person's filthy was another person's tolerable, but they ran their budget and realized that they could easily afford having a housecleaner tidy up their home maybe once a month. So they hired one. And that was the end of the issue. Of course, not all of us have the privilege to throw money at our problems or necessary tasks that we don't want to do, but at the same time, many of those tasks might be more affordable than you think, if you're willing to compromise with yourself on them. So maybe you don't pick up your kid from school every day, but your neighbor who also picks up a child at the same time would be willing to pick up yours in exchange for a batch of brownies every month or something along those lines. Maybe instead of doing your laundry every week, you buy a few extra pairs of pants and underwear and do it every two weeks or send your laundry out for cleaning instead, even if it costs a bit of money. See where I'm going? Expand those possibilities, and even if they don't pan out, at least you'll know where you can and can't be flexible.

3. IS THERE ANY WAY TO MAKE THIS TAKE LESS TIME?

Now it's time to see if you can do these things without spending the time you normally would spend on them. As I said, consider enlisting help from someone else or spreading the load of the job over more time. Perhaps with better tools or a different approach, what you're working on would take less time than it currently does. Again, throwing a little money at the problem might help—after all, vacuuming with a DustBuster is going to take way more time than it would using a proper standing or stick vacuum. Money doesn't have to be the fix, though. Other times it's just about modernizing your approach or taking advantage of another approach. If you're spending time running to and from the post office, maybe it's worth learning to print off your own mailing labels and connecting with your letter carriers so they can take your outgoing parcels for you when they pick up your mail. These are a few semi-obvious examples, but the key is to think about how you can get the same results with a slightly different—and ideally more efficient—approach to these must-do tasks. The trick here is to take a step back and give the same level of thought into your personal time management as you give your work time management. And sometimes that means talking to friends and family about taking some time back from their expectations of you, too.

4. IS THERE ANY WAY TO MAKE THIS EASIER?

Finally, your next question should be a simple one: Can you make this task, which needs to get done, less intensive? Not necessarily less time-intensive, but less effort-inducing, less troublesome, and less deserving of being on the must-do list and more like something you can put on the want-to-do list. Maybe you don't dislike the task, but it becomes a chore because of how you have to do it or how often you have to do it. There are definitely issues to consider when it comes to cutting corners. But if you can find a technique that stands by your ethics, is good for you, and makes a chore easier so you don't have to think about it or devote as much time to it, then you should use that technique.

PRODUCTIVITY METHODS
ARE MEANT TO WORK FOR YOU

Those must-do tasks are the ones best suited to the hacks and the productivity techniques. When I'm overwhelmed and have too much on my plate, I often forget what I'm supposed to do next, because I'm hyperfocused on whatever I'm working on at the moment—or what I've just finished. That's where keeping a simple to-do list comes in. It offloads that work to an app, so I don't have to waste time or energy keeping track. When I have to write or edit, it's sometimes difficult to get into the work, even when I know I have to. Sure, I can do plenty of things to get into the emotional space conducive to work, but once I get started, I tend to use a method like the pomodoro technique, which I mentioned earlier, to give myself regular breathers while still carving out time for dedicated work. This technique helps me at least to know that I have a break coming up where I can indulge my distracted mind if necessary and that all I need to do is keep writing for a little longer until the break time. Also helping take the pressure off my already-stressed brain is knowing I can offload to an app even the job of remembering the stuff I have to do. When you have the added pressure of navigating the world as a marginalized person, every little bit helps.

Many common productivity techniques, including David Allen's GTD method, the pomodoro technique, and the kanban method, all have elements that work for different types of workers, from creatives to project-oriented people to developers and techies. That's the basics of productivity. But for workers who struggle with their own productivity at the office, especially those who face discrimination or prejudice, the key is to mix and match elements from multiple techniques that work best for you. For example, if you don't have heads-down work sessions that you can dive into and then briefly escape for a short break, then the pomodoro technique probably wouldn't work well for you. If your boss or colleagues have no respect for your time and book you for meetings over some scheduled work sessions you already have marked on your shared calendar, then *time blocking* won't work for you. (With this productivity method, you carve out your workday into dedicated times for specific tasks, for example, a chunk in the morning for documentation, a time in the late morning for deep work, and a time in the afternoon for meetings.) If you're free from those prejudices, you can put those techniques to work in a way that benefits you.

But here's the thing: You don't have to use any one method and feel locked into it, and just because a method won't work for you doesn't mean that you can't borrow some elements from it and put them into practice along with other techniques. In my personal experience, I've taken the best of kanban, a very visual productivity method that uses sticky notes, or an app like Trello, a popular to-do and project-tracking tool, to keep track of the things I have to work on. I then move the tasks from one column to another as they go from the idea stage to the working stage and finally to the completed stage. I combined my system with the punctual, top-down nature of the GTD productivity method and the rotating work/ break focus of pomodoro to be a better writer without losing touch of the people who need to get ahold of me when they reach out. The key is to distill the most popular methods into portable, useful tips that can be used across industries and positions and then apply the ones that work while discarding the additional weight that may not apply. Charts 1 and 2 list some popular productivity techniques or applications.

CHART 1: POPULAR PRODUCTIVITY METHODS

GTD	Pomodoro Technique
Popularized by David Allen in his book *Getting Things Done*, this method focuses on off-boarding tasks to to-do lists and reminders, prioritizing tasks efficiently, and only spending time on what's doable. It requires time to implement, including an hour-long weekly review, but no monetary cost (aside from his book).	Developed in the 1980s by Francesco Cirillo, this method is favored by developers and consistent-output workers who can focus on a single task for short periods. This method involves working in short, focused bursts (25:5 x 4) and then taking breaks to recharge. All you need is a timer, and the freedom to structure your work to fit the method.
Kaizen	Personal Kanban
Translated as "get better and getting better," this is a philosophy more than a method. It focuses on finding new and continual ways to improve at every opportunity. This method is collaborative and requires as much time as you allow.	Developed by Jim Benson and Tonianne DeMaria Barry, this highly visual method of organization gives you a bird's-eye view of your actionable to-dos and how they fit into a bigger picture. You can use free or paid apps, sticky notes, or a dry-erase board for this purpose. Setup time is required, but little else.

DBTC	The Action Method
The Don't Break the Chain method helps you build positive feedback loops and better habits. Choose a task you want to complete regularly, mark it on a calendar each time you do it, and use the visual motivation to continue.	Developed by the social media platform Behance for creatives, this method emphasizes actionable to-dos from every task, project, or goal, and incremental progress. Behance sells notebooks, but they're not required.

CHART 2: A SELECTION OF POPULAR PRODUCTIVITY APPS

Manage Tasks or To-Dos	Manage Whole Projects	Manage Ideas
Todoist, Microsoft To Do, Google Keep, TickTick, Any.do, Clear Todos, Reminders, Carrot, Remember the Milk, Toodledo	Trello, Things, Asana, OmniFocus and OmniPlan, Airtable, Evernote	Asana, Evernote, Google Keep, Notational Velocity, Simplenote, Pen and Paper

Collaborate	Focus; Avoid Distractions	Remember to Take Breaks!
Airtable, Asana, Trello, Slack, Discord	SelfControl (Mac), Freedom (PC), RescueTime, Concentrate (Mac), WriteRoom, StayFocusd	Time Out (Mac), Rest (Mac), Breaker (PC), Workrave (PC), Coffee Break (Mac)

So how does that work, exactly? I like to keep track of my ideas in one tool and my to-dos in another. Many people might consider this approach too complicated and would prefer one app to meet their needs, but when I was working at *Lifehacker* and got to testing out multiple apps and services, I found myself falling in love with more than one method. Call it my own productivity porn indulgence. (Sorry, Vivek!) So I keep my ideas and broad project thoughts in a very kanban-style setup, where I can move them around columns like Planning, Next on Deck, Working, Finishing Touches, and Done. That's just for ideas, though—it gives me a way to clearly see what I'm working on at a high level. And if, for example, my priorities change, I can move a Next on Deck task back to Planning, so I don't feel bad about not starting the task.

My actual to-do list is in an app designed explicitly for specific tasks: It notifies me when the task is due, and when I complete it, I mark it off. I try to keep ideas and broad projects out of my to-do app unless I've taken the time to break the project down into action-able steps. Breaking down projects into small chunks, by the way, is a critical characteristic of GTD, as is making sure you always have a top-level view of everything you're doing (and why, as we'll explain later). So much of GTD is designed to keep you focused on *why* you're doing the work you do, so you don't get lost in it and lose that precious time you could be spending on your passion projects or other things you like to do.

Then, once I have my actionable tasks and steps, I apply the pomodoro method to them, focusing on deep work in bursts and then coming up for breaks periodically to keep my mind refreshed and to stay as productive on those tasks as possible. I even borrow from the time-blocking method (although not rigidly) because I know my best working hours are later in the day. I save those hours for brain-intensive work, like writing or editing, and I spend my less productive and less energetic hours on more menial tasks like following up on email and scheduling meetings. But I rarely block the time off on my calendar unless I really need to, partly because I'm so used to people booking something for a period that I already have booked (although, to be fair, my colleagues now aren't like that).

That's my approach, a method that works for me. It's more complicated than I'd normally recommend for people who just need to keep track of their projects at work, for those who need essentially a chore wheel at home, and especially for marginalized people who want a way to release some of the pressure building up in their inboxes and work assignments. But even so, it's complicated because throughout my career in journalism, and even when I was a project manager, I had very little control over my schedule and had to accept meetings whenever they landed. In one case, I was so marginalized that declining a meeting or asking to move it around meant the risk of not having the opportunity to participate at all or, worse, just being totally excluded. In another case, I was in such high demand that I was booked all the time; trying to carve out time for myself was an impossible task when the calendar was as full as mine was.

The bottom line, though, is that my complicated system was born out of my having to adjust how I worked because of being marginalized or discriminated against in some way. When the microaggressions in the form of complaints that I wasn't getting back to people fast enough became more than I could bear, I started handling emails en masse the first thing in the morning and making sure that I could always see the bottom of my in-box. A lot of people don't, and don't have to, but I was actively being sidelined and considered lazy and disengaged if I didn't respond quickly. I learned to glance at new email notifications on my phone and judge their importance because if I didn't, someone would be tapping a foot somewhere wondering why I hadn't responded yet and why I was obviously so bad at prioritizing. If any of this sounds familiar to you as someone who's also marginalized at work, you know what I mean—and there's absolutely no shame in borrowing only parts of a productivity method rather than using the entire method, even if the creator begs you to. You need to create a system that works exclusively for you, the way you work, and the expectations you're under.

Now let's go back to your second list, the one where you wrote down everything that you're truly passionate about. This is where you make sure that you make time for those things too—after all, I wouldn't be giving you proper productivity advice if I only focused on helping you do the stuff you don't want to do. Luckily, I have one specific tip for taking care of the second list, and we'll look at this tip next.

EMBRACE THE WEEKLY REVIEW

Here's all you have to do to make sure the items on your want-to-do list don't fall by the wayside: Conduct a good weekly review. Every week, maybe on Friday or Monday, book yourself for an hour's meeting. No attendees, just you. (I prefer Friday afternoons, which are usually slow enough to allow me to set aside this hour, because everyone's trying to leave for the weekend.) If your desk or office is too noisy, try to find a quiet spot where you can relax a little bit, and take your laptop. If you have to sit at your desk, put on a pair of headphones (consider noise-canceling headphones for the office; I recommend them wholeheartedly) to block out the rest of the world.

I wish I could say I created this idea, but I can't. This productivity technique comes from David Allen—again, from *Getting Things Done*—but it's a single action, not a whole system. It's called the *weekly review,* and I swear by it and wish more people, especially marginalized folks, used it as well. This hour is just for you. In fact, the point of this hour-long session is to *not* do work. This is time for you to get out in front of your to-dos at work and at home and to try to get a broad perspective of everything on your plate. The other point of this exercise is to spend a little time thinking about how you can work smarter.

Okay, once you have a little isolation and you can focus, get into the mood. Maybe grab some water or stretch a bit before you begin. After all, this exercise is a good thing, and you should enjoy doing it. This is why I tend to schedule mine for Fridays—it's a bit of a celebration of all the work I've done over the week and a little organizational prep for the week to come, with a nice, healthy weekend break in between. Now at this point, Allen says that you should focus on three objectives during your weekly review: getting clear, getting current, and getting creative.[1] Let's touch on each one at a time.

GET CLEAR

Getting clear means that this hour-long session is your opportunity to sweep clean the debris of the previous week. It's a good time to clean out your in-box if you can—and by clean out, I mean archive or delete messages, set their priority, change their tags or however else you would organize them, but not replying to them or starting new conversations. After all, you don't want to spend this hour *doing work*. This is purely organizational time, so it's also a good chance to catch up on any documentation you were supposed to read and familiarize yourself with; organize any loose paperwork, materials, or tools that you use for your job (now is a good time to clean the paintbrushes, for example!); and generally organize your area if you like an organized workspace. The bottom line is that in getting clear, you can kind of empty your in-box, clean up your space, empty your head, and try to decompress a bit from the events of the week. It's meant to be a time when you're less focused on the nuts and bolts of your work and more focused on what your work means, both to you and to your employer. You think about how much time and energy you spend on your work and whether that matches up with its level of importance, again, to you and to your employer.

GET CURRENT

Getting current is the meat of your weekly review. Take the time to look at your calendar, and review the meetings you had this week. Ask yourself a few questions, and note the answers:

- What happened in your meetings this week?
- Did you move things forward, or was it just a bunch of people talking in a circle?
- What actionable tasks came out of it for you, and how are those going ahead of the next meeting?
- Review your to-do list. Is everything that you actually need to do on there? If not, now is a great time to add anything you've been meaning to or anything that came out of the events of the past week that you haven't remembered to add.
- What projects are you working on, and what's their status, if anyone should ask you?

This part of the weekly review is a good opportunity to stop and think about those things you would tell someone if they asked you, "So, what are you working on?"

But don't forget to look forward as well. Here are a few more things to ask yourself:

- What's on your plate for the following week?
- Are there any meetings coming up that you need to prepare for or projects launching next week that you want to be a part of (but which you would have to fight for or be strategic to score an invitation to)?

- Are there any events next week that you're looking forward to or blocks in your schedule that you can cordon off for things you want to do?

- Can you make any changes now to make that first list a little easier to manage, or can you pull anything off the list entirely? Now is a great time to think about that as well. This is also when you'll think about anything you would have done this week except that you're waiting on someone else to provide something, like a status update, a missing part, or a shipment you've been tracking.

- And finally, look at the work you're doing, and try to fit it into those overall, larger priorities. Does the work you're doing right now even matter?

Ask yourself these questions and answer them for yourself and for your manager or the company. This way, you know exactly what you're looking forward to in the coming days or weeks, and you can consider those events in the context of the social baggage you already carry and your relationship with your colleagues. If you know that someone will work hard to marginalize you, you have an opportunity well in advance to consider your strategy to counter their actions. If someone dominates meetings, making it hard for you to talk with a colleague you'd like to work with, you can now think about scheduling a coffee with this colleague well in advance, so that you can be proactive instead of reactive.

Reframe your level of effort and energy to align with the things that actually matter, if you can. That's the core of getting current—it means you're mentally caught up with the work you're doing instead of suffering psychologically under the avalanche of tasks and to-dos. You're not just aware of the individual tasks but also aware of how they fit into broader projects and goals. You know whether the energy you put into those tasks lines up with what matters to your boss, or even to you, and you make an active decision to accept that or change it.

GET CREATIVE

Now here's where things get fun. *Getting creative* is your time to brainstorm. Think about big projects you'd like to work on, ideas you'd like to get off the ground. For marginalized workers, getting creative means thinking about the things you really want to be a part of but have been excluded from for whatever reason. For me, the idea for the article that inspired this book, and indeed even the book proposal itself, came to me during my creative time. This is your chance to reach out and schedule coffees with people with whom you'd like to work or managers who run departments you'd rather join. When you get creative, you begin thinking about your dream projects, like starting that company newsletter that you'll write every week, joining (or creating!) the employee resource group for people like you at your company, or giving a presentation at an industry conference about the work you do.

Get creative and be brave: Make your "I'd like to do this someday" list, and it doesn't necessarily have to be stuff you can do at work or even at this job. Be bold. Getting creative is exactly your time to do that: to broaden your horizons and think openly about what your life would look like if you only had that first list to work on, the one full of things you actually want to do.

A typical weekly review would go something like fifteen minutes on getting clear, thirty on getting current, and another fifteen on getting creative. As you get the methodology down, you can shift those around however you like, but they're a good baseline. Also, as I established earlier, the weekly review isn't a time for doing work. It might be tempting, since you'll probably uncover a bunch of tasks that you need to do—phone calls to make, emails to send, follow-ups you intended to do but forgot—that's all okay. Add them to your to-do list, and tackle them next week, organized, along with everything else. Allen's rule here is that if the task takes less than two minutes, go ahead and do it during your review, but if it will take longer than two minutes, add it to your to-do list and save it for later. You don't want to spend your precious review time doing the work you're supposed to be getting away from and getting a top-down view of.

The first or second time you conduct your weekly review might feel a little like you're planning to plan, which is okay. Push through that initial feeling, unless your job type really isn't the kind that would benefit from a weekly review. It's definitely a productivity technique that works best for office workers, creatives, and people who have to juggle multiple priorities but who also work with computers or at desks and such. If you work in a warehouse, for example, or in customer service, you don't need to spend an hour organizing if you know next week will be more of exactly the same thing you do this week—but I'd argue that even in those cases, you can benefit from a dedicated time to think big and dream about where you could go if you applied yourself and your skills in a different way. And that dedicated thinking time speaks to some of the benefits of doing the weekly review regularly: You'll always have that top-down, 10,000-foot view of your work and how it fits into the team and the company. You'll always know exactly how much bandwidth you have to spare, both at work and in your personal life. You'll always find yourself working with the knowledge that what you're doing is either the best use of your skills or a waste of your time—the glamour work or the housework. And perhaps most important, you'll have a little mental space away from the grinding day-to-day to make sure that you're not just working your skills, but you're also being creative and looking for ways to empower yourself either at work or somewhere else. That alone means a lot.

ALWAYS BE CAPTURING (IDEAS)

Kadavy offered me one more tip that I think applies to just about everyone, whether you're the type of person to do the weekly review or not: Think about how you can save your mental energy for the things that matter—the things you're hoping to have time for by doing your weekly review. "Another way to get more out of your mental energy on your glamour projects is ABC: Not 'Always Be Closing,' like in *Glengarry Glen Ross*," Kadavy explained. "Instead, Always Be Capturing. Ideas come at random, and they rarely come at the right time—especially when the time you get to dedicate to glamour projects is limited. When, while working on a grunt task, you get an idea for one of your glamour projects, stop and jot it down. (If you do this on your phone, it will look like you're texting, so get a pocket notebook and collapsible pen to use when grunt work takes you away from your keyboard.)" That last bit is especially useful for marginalized folks—raise your hand if you've ever gotten dirty looks because you were on your phone or using your laptop during a meeting and someone assumed that it was because you were goofing off, as opposed to taking notes.

"When you do get a moment to work on a glamour project,"

Kadavy said, "review the ideas in this 'in-box.' Transfer them to a central place related to the project and develop those ideas bit by bit in those in-between moments during which you get to think creatively. You'll have better ideas, they'll come easily, and you'll do it all with very little active time invested." I can't think of a better way to get things done than to spend at least some time making sure that you save your energy for the things that are most important to you.

RULE 11

Always Look Busy

(FOCUSING ON THE IMPORTANT WORK)

know this rule seems to contradict the earlier one about being productive and not busy, but there are moments when, if you're a marginalized worker, it's best to look busy to avoid having someone else's busywork or office housework thrust on you. And what's more important, to someone with prejudices (malice) or someone who just hasn't interrogated their own social programming (ignorance), a marginalized person who has things under control can look not busy or, worse, lazy.

Alternatively, if you have a handle on your work and you are an essential person who's respected and appreciated, it's also nice to know when to look busy so that you are left alone with your work. If you earn the burden of being in high demand, people eager to leverage your skills will be in your email in-box or standing at your desk looking to "pick your brain." In some cases, those can be great projects to work on and great people to connect and work with. In other cases, however, those people will be looking to make you do work on their behalf while they happily take credit for it, or they want you to take ownership of something problematic or difficult so you can work yourself to the bone salvaging it or at the very least be forced to take ownership when it fails.

When you're already marginalized—for example, you're the only woman in an office full of frat boys—you should expect that at least some of the projects someone may come to you with aren't so much designed to make you shine but are used to cover someone else's ass. I hate to be fatalistic, and I hope that everyone has the opportunity to work in a place where their skills and their time are valued, but I know that's a rare privilege. So until we all have that opportunity, sometimes the best way to protect your boundaries when you're in high demand is to look busier than you are (this is also the best way to protect yourself from being tagged lazy).

I'm not kidding. It's often better to be perceived as a person who always has their eyes on what's happening than the person actually losing sleep because you are the one watching everything. Part of this is quietly and privately picking and choosing the projects you spend the most time on and making sure that you pay just enough attention to other things that you have deniable reasons and explanations should someone come asking after them. I know, I know, this sounds underhanded and kind of sketchy, but just remember two things: First of all, one person's sketchy is another person's life hack. Second, I guarantee that some people in your office are managing their workloads in exactly this manner and are absolutely unguarded in discussing it as just another way they keep everything together and stay organized.

Let's consider email as an example. In just about every job, it's important to keep an eye on your in-box so you know who's emailing you about what, but it's less important to respond quickly to everyone with a detailed status update. Being able to carefully choose who needs attention is essential. But being able to tell someone that you're already aware of the issue or task they're reaching out about (even if you don't have an answer for them yet) is also enough for some of those people. More of your coworkers will appreciate your telling them—either in person or in an email—"Yup, I saw your email and I'm looking into the issue" instead of telling them to their face later, after they've been waiting for a follow-up, "I saw your email, but I haven't had time to look into it yet."

MIND MANAGEMENT, NOT TIME MANAGEMENT

I reached back out to Kadavy for some concrete tips on how to look busy, whether you are busy or not. His most recent book, *Mind Management, Not Time Management,* touches on a lot of these same topics, including how to make sure you save mental space for what is most important to you, instead of just spinning your wheels. And sure enough, his first tip was good, important, and along those lines: Save your mental energy as much as possible, especially on those housework tasks and to-dos that don't advance your career.

"Each time you do one of these tasks, jot down quick notes about the process you followed," Kadavy explained. "The next time you do that same task, take out your notes, and add to or refine the process you've written. Eventually you'll have clearly defined steps or even a checklist. From then on, every time you do the task, just follow the checklist. Not only does this make mindless tasks truly mindless—it also eliminates errors that could tarnish your reputation." It's true—part of looking busy is making sure you know what to spend your time on, what deserves less time but has to be done anyway, and, between the two, which deserves your full attention as opposed to simply going through the motions.

And Kadavy doesn't just suggest you do this at work, either. "It seems pointless to write down the steps you follow to, say, make breakfast, but doing so is revealing. How many times have you sat down to breakfast and realized you forgot a spoon? If you write down the steps, you're forced to think about how the perfect time to grab a spoon is right after you take a bowl out of the cupboard and place it on the countertop, and right before you remove the cereal box from the other cupboard. It's not like you wake up in the morning and don't know how to make breakfast, but when you formalize, then follow the same steps a few times, they get programmed into your mind so it's automatic—like the steps of a dance or tying your shoes."

During my time as a project manager and while I was the editor in chief of *Lifehacker*, I was deluged with email that I had to respond to as soon as possible. You'd think being a *Times* journalist would have been overwhelming too, and while I definitely got a lot of email during those years, it wasn't unmanageable. It was the project management gig that drove the most email: people wanting status updates, copies of our project plans, meeting minutes, and long threads about changing some nuance of an ongoing project or budgetary issues would pile up, even overnight, to welcome me in the morning. I don't say all of this just to flex—I'm sure some of you reading this would certainly win should we compare in-boxes—but one thing was absolutely certain: I had to be *aware* of everything happening in my mailbox without being *distracted* by it.

So even if someone caught me in an elevator in between meetings and said, "I sent you an email a little while ago. Did you see it?"

it would be perfectly okay to say, "No, sorry, I was in a meeting." But it's far more empowering—and it buys you more time—if you can say, "I saw, but I haven't had a chance to look at it yet. What did you say?"

You can see how there's nothing wrong with the former response, but the latter gives you more flexibility and offers the other person an opportunity to immediately distill for you what they need. This response can save you time later, if you even need to reply after you've spoken. And while the second option keeps you on top of a potential change to your workload, it also shows others that you have things together and you're prepared at any time to discuss what they need and what you can do.

Of course, all of this advice applies regardless of whether you're actually ready to discuss it and whether you have the bandwidth to take on their request. You just have to be able to think on your feet enough to give them an answer in person that lets you buy the time or separation necessary to look into their issue later. This tip goes into the same category of office tips like "always have something to say when someone asks you what you're working on," or "always have something to talk about if you get stuck in an elevator with an executive." Tips like these may sound simplistic, but if you can get past the "Ew, business speak" nature of the advice, you can use it as an opportunity to truly connect with someone else or speak competently about the nature of your work. You'll also do yourself a huge favor when it comes to looking busy and looking as if you have a lot on your plate. And finally, you'll look like you have a handle on it because you're a capable and competent worker.

BETTER TO BE RESPECTED THAN LIKED

Remember, looking competent is only part of the goal here. You also want to make sure that you look *busy*. You'll want to appear maxed out on bandwidth but not frenetic or stressed, even if you are—ostensibly firing on all cylinders. And to do that, you need to leverage some of the same productivity tricks that you normally couldn't use because of the social baggage you're carrying around with you but that you tweaked so they work for you, not against you. I asked Adam Grant about this as well when we were talking about being a people pleaser and the right way to say no to requests for work. He reminded me of something important: So often, we focus on looking busy because we want to be liked and well regarded in the workplace, and sometimes, especially for marginalized people, that desire can backfire.

"One of the systematic mistakes that people seem to make is that they want to be liked instead of respected. Saying yes to everyone is a great way to make people like you. It is not going to guarantee that anyone respects you. I think, especially if you're highly agreeable like me—and I get the sense that you are—the yes is like, 'I want to please everyone; I don't want to say no.'" I agreed with him on both points. I'm also absolutely a person who wants to please everyone at work and who often finds himself taking on extra work for bad reasons, like wanting to be liked.

But Grant reminded me, "You're not there to please everyone; you're there to make people better. That's a different set of rules about when to say yes and when to say no, and it requires more nos."

This reminded me of a colleague in the newsroom who used to keep a day booked from top to bottom on his calendar and usually labeled it "No-Meeting Day." For a long time, it was Tuesday, just because "no-meeting Tuesday" rolled off the tongue. In fact, it was that colleague making such good use of that productivity tip—a tip I know I've written about at *Lifehacker* long before I made it to the *Times*—that in some ways inspired this book. I realized that our colleagues, by default, respected his approach. He would occasionally have to defend it, telling people that he wouldn't accept meeting requests during those days and that the rest of his calendar was up-to-date so they could find another time to meet. In other cases, he'd ignore the meeting request entirely and just not show up and miss the meeting. And while all those things were *fine*, they're technically infractions that would get other employees not fired, perhaps, but certainly not respected as a maverick capable of effectively managing their time.

I thought back to my time as a project manager and knowing that even though I had a leadership role on my team, if someone wanted to meet at a given time, hitting the Decline button simply wasn't an option. I had other concerns to worry about: Would the person who wanted the meeting go and speak to my manager? Would they complain that I'm not a team player or that I'm difficult to work with? Instead of understanding that I just needed that time for something else, would they think that I'm not good at managing my workflow or, worse, that they just weren't important to me and feel slighted, professionally?

Fast-forward to the *Times* again, and I was in a similar boat. My colleague and I were peers, but I could tell the difference in our interactions immediately: If I declined a meeting, the reaction was "Something's wrong, and I'm being inconvenienced" or "Something's wrong, and I'm inconveniencing him," instead of the assumption "Oh, he's busy." Choosing to attend a meeting wasn't a power play for me; it was a basic job requirement. If I skipped a meeting, I'd hear about it later. No one, not one person, assumed that I missed the meeting, or booked a whole day on my calendar, because I needed to focus on a task or actually do my work. That's if they assumed anything at all. More often than not, if someone wanted to meet with me, my calendar was more of a guideline than a rule: They'd just book over any existing appointments I had and let me figure it out.

RULE 12

Protect Yourself

(TRACKING YOUR WORK)

S itting across from my manager during a one-on-one after several months of trying to work up the courage to discuss a concern, I finally explained to her that I thought I wasn't getting the same resources that my colleagues were getting. I cited a recent example of a colleague—less experienced than I but definitely louder—who had been actively keeping me from a new audience-focused project, a newsletter, where our readers could get to know us and our team, and where we could highlight a lot of the great stories we were publishing. When I asked to be involved, he would nod and agree to my face, but when it came time to actually help out, there was never a good opportunity. The one time I did get a chance to help, I was heavily curtailed, and the project was so rushed that I didn't even get a byline. After that one time, I never got to participate again.

My colleague was so possessive of the project that he chose to hire other people to write it when he needed gaps filled rather than let me help. He would write it on vacation before letting me help. He would turn it around far too late for the people who needed to take his copy and set it up to send out. These people would then come to me asking if I could do anything to make the process work better, even though I was being intentionally excluded from the process. But beyond all that, my colleague was clearly playing favorites with this project, and once it became a powerful way to promote and boost the work we were doing, suddenly anything I had been working on wound up excluded from the newsletter. And between not being included in the newsletter and not getting the same level of social promotion, I didn't have the same levers to pull to make sure the work I was doing got the same exposure in our community. And, of course, that lack of exposure made the work I was doing appear less valuable and less worthwhile.

I urged my manager to step in and do something. I explained that this was part of a pattern that had been going on for months, possibly over a year: I was being purposefully excluded from valuable projects and initiatives, sidelined and marginalized, excluded from meetings that I could have been an active participant in and projects I would have liked to lead. She smiled and laughed along with me when I joked about the situation, but the bottom line from her was that she was sympathetic but couldn't do anything about it unless it was definitely a pattern that was actively harming my work.

And that's where I'd gone wrong. I had been seething and had plenty of examples in my head, but I hadn't written anything down. I lacked the data to support my complaints, even if it was obvious that what I was saying was true and problematic. At the end of the day, though, I believe that it would have taken a good bit of data to prompt her into action, because she was conflict-averse (perhaps as much as I am) and politically savvy (which I don't blame her for, considering she had managed to survive in that environment long enough to be a senior manager). While she privately wished the situation were better for me, there was little she could do without rocking enough boats that doing so would be troublesome. After our conversation, I was happy that at least my manager was privately in my corner. But I was still frustrated that, publicly, the result was that I was still on the outside looking in on my own team, trying desperately to jump in on opportunities to actually do my job instead of just sit at my desk and twiddle my thumbs all day, which I suppose I should have been happy to do.

But with this interaction, I learned one important lesson: Managers, HR departments, and companies can all ignore complaints; they can ignore reports of harassment and marginalization; and they can even ignore you, specifically, and avoid working with you or integrating you with their team. But there's one thing they can't ignore or at least have more difficulty ignoring: data.

Or more precisely, it's harder to dismiss your concerns about being marginalized and excluded from projects, events, or even whole teams or doing all the office housework instead of getting the glamour opportunities that would let you advance your career, if you have data (a record) to back up your claims. And by data, I don't mean numbers like general statistics, although those can be helpful to have as a backup, more industry-wide issue. But no manager is going to be convinced that they're marginalizing their only female employee, their only disabled employee, or their only Muslim employee because of national data that proves that such problems are happening around the country or even around the world. As always, the statistical is generally accepted as true, but it's the anecdotal that forces people into action in their own lives.

KEEP TRACK OF YOUR WORK

So for you, protecting yourself from marginalization means keeping track of the work you've been assigned and the work you've missed out on. It means keeping track of who's doing what and building your case over time for exactly how you've been marginalized and what impact it has had on you. I know, like some of the other techniques we've discussed here, this recommendation sounds like an additional job: keeping track of what everyone else is doing in addition to what you're doing. But don't think too deeply about it, and don't get too resentful of having to do it. In the end, the tracking will empower you more than add to your plate. Everyone in virtually every job should keep close track of their successes, failures, opportunities and who those opportunities eventually went to, and what they learned from their accomplishments and failures.

"My recommendation is to start listing out details of assignments by date, time, assignment type, who assigned it, and how much presumed time it would take . . . and as much other detail as possible," Ruchika Tulshyan explained to me. When I wrote about being discriminated against at work and how I found success regardless, not only did Tulshyan help with actionable advice to include in my article, but her suggestions and her stories were also a bit of a balm for me.[1] Talking to her about what I'd experienced and working with her to come up with ideas so other people didn't have to go through the same thing didn't just inform an article and start a friendship but also inspired this book. She continued, "A spreadsheet or handwritten ledger will do. It will also help illuminate [the answer to this question]: Is office housework unfairly assigned, or do some people volunteer for it? I think this really helps in instances of gaslighting or when you're told, 'Oh, it was just a one-off.'"

And that's exactly the problem I ran into: My manager thought that the issue was a one-off or that even if it was a pattern of behavior, it was only with regard to one element of my work and not to my job as a whole. I didn't have the data to communicate that not only was my colleague marginalizing me from this one thing, but he was also marginalizing me (and other people he didn't care for, like our poor editorial assistant, who had to bear the brunt of his bad behavior) from virtually everything. The fact that managers see problems like this so narrowly, perhaps intentionally to avoid taking action, is a lesson I won't forget, and I hope you'll never have to learn.

Part of learning to keep track of your work builds on making the weekly review a habit. Once you set aside a regular time to review your work and why you're doing it, it's easy to start making a list of the things you're doing and the opportunities you've both scored and missed out on, and why. It's a way to be heard.

After all, this information is likely to be fresher in your mind at the end of a given week than it would be months later. And this data may also help you build that case for proving to your manager—or HR or anyone else who asks—that you're being marginalized or saddled with the housework and denied opportunities to let your skills shine. When you do sit down to that meeting with your manager or another authority to explain that what you're going through at work isn't fair or right, you'll have ammunition.

Tulshyan explained, "I would recommend that it [the data] be available in the first meeting you're raising concerns, whether with your manager or another leader or HR. It is really important to be able to say, 'I was asked to [order], and ordered, lunch four times in the past few meetings. Here are the instances. I want to be a team player, and I also know that always completing these tasks can disproportionately impact my chance of advancement. Can we re-distribute this work?'"

But keeping track of your work doesn't just help convince other people to treat you fairly when they wouldn't otherwise. It also helps you—or, rather, the future you.

KEEP YOUR RÉSUMÉ UPDATED, AND START A WORK DIARY

Too often, once we land a new job, we assume everything is great and stop updating our résumé. You know the honeymoon period at a new job, where you're fresh off feeling wanted because you actually got the job and you're in now, learning the ropes and trying to figure out how to best work with your new team? It's a busy period, for sure, but it's important to update your résumé as soon as you land a new job, and then keep it up-to-date during that honeymoon period, when you're still thrilled to go to work every day. It's not so much in case you have to leave all of a sudden, but you should keep good track of what you're working on, what you're assigned, and where your biggest and brightest ideas go in those early days. Having a record of all this information makes it easier for you in the long run.

Keeping track of your ideas, projects, and wins helps in other areas of your career as well. You'll always have a long list of things to talk to your manager about when you can compare what you're working on with what you wish you were working on, for example. This information is also really helpful when you interview with other companies or network with other people in your industry and they ask you about the work you've been doing.

So let's get right to it: Consider keeping a work diary.[2] It's a bit of a living memoir of your accomplishments and your work experiences. It's also a place for you to keep track of the things that happen in meetings, for example, when the loudest person in the room is the one who scores that great assignment, and when no one raises a hand to volunteer to take the meeting minutes, so your boss just asks you to do it again. A work diary is also a great sanity check on whether you really are being assigned the less glamourous work and being sidelined more than others. Finally, it gives you useful, empirical information to present to managers at performance reviews, one-on-ones, and other meetings where you raise your concerns or have an opportunity to talk about your successes and goals.

IT'S CATHARTIC TO KEEP TRACK OF YOUR WINS AND YOUR LOSSES

There's another benefit to keeping a work diary: It's cathartic. I can't overstate that enough. There's something powerful about not only writing down your experiences when things go right in your job but also writing down the opportunities that you've been denied and how you'd handle them, even if the record is just for yourself. It helps you process the emotions of being marginalized: the isolation, the loneliness, the anger, and the resentment. There's also power in writing down what you *would* have done if you had been given the opportunity, because then at your next job, you can put these ideas into motion. For example, sure you may have been sidelined for the writing project that went to your less experienced peer, and sure you probably would have handled it differently from the way he did. But when you interview for your next job, you can point out that you have this great writing idea and outline all the ways you would and could handle it if they offered you the position.

So how do you keep a work diary, exactly? That part is a bit less important than you may think, as long as you make sure that you jot down all the important things I've mentioned. Whether it's a simple text file on your computer, a file you keep in the cloud so that you can access and update it from multiple computers, or a paper journal that you can carry around between meetings and enjoy writing in, it doesn't totally matter what form your work diary takes. It should simply be something that you'll want to regularly update and feel good about using.

I keep my work diary in a Google Docs document associated with one of my personal accounts. Because it's not connected directly to any account I have with an employer, I don't have to worry about losing access to it if I change jobs. Nor do I have to use a company computer to access it. I can download it freely and can access it on any computer or smartphone I feel comfortable logging in on. If you wouldn't trust Google with that information, a simple text file on your computer will do just fine. Some people prefer to keep a physical journal and then use it not only to keep track of events at work but also to record their projects, ideas, and to-dos. After all, if you do keep everything organized in some form of work diary, it's a single place to turn to when you conduct your weekly review or if you need fodder to update your résumé or prepare for an interview.

Some people prefer to use a spreadsheet for their work diary, keeping rows for assignments and lessons learned and columns for the date, whether you got the assignment, or other useful notes. You could even use the spreadsheet for your projects, keeping a separate tab in the spreadsheet for lessons learned from each project, the names of projects or events you were excluded from, and the reasons the excluders gave you, along with what you could have brought to the table if you hadn't been excluded in the first place.

THE ESSENTIALS TO TRACK

How you organize your work diary is up to you as well. But there are a few important things to keep track of:

- The things you're working on and your successes.
- The small wins, especially if you know your manager won't sing your praises. It's important to celebrate the small wins.
- Your struggles or the challenges you're tackling (just in case you ever walk into an interview and someone asks you, "Tell me about a time you struggled or a challenge you overcame").
- The work you've either missed out on because you were excluded or were passed over for because you were being marginalized.

The bottom line is that collecting this kind of information, whatever form it may take, is your best weapon against allowing the loudest person in the room to dominate, pretend (at best) or lie (at worst) about their importance, or assign themselves glamour work while leaving office housekeeping in the air for others. You need this information especially if you hesitate to challenge that behavior when it's happening. And besides, if you're already often discriminated against at work, for whatever reason that may be, jumping in at the moment can already be problematic. So this information gives you an option to push back against that social conditioning and the privilege your colleague is wielding. Make no mistake, having this data at your fingertips is a powerful tool, and even if your manager or their boss won't listen to it, you'll have essential information you can use for future endeavors. And that's perhaps even more valuable than your boss's efforts to shoehorn you into a project where someone else is actively trying to keep you out.

When I spoke with Tulshyan about my experience of being locked out of an opportunity for the long haul for no real reason other than my colleague's ego, I asked if she had encountered any issues similar in her career and, if so, how she challenged them. "I would say that my big regret is never feeling safe to bring up issues of office housework in a corporate setting, and so I never really did," Tulshyan told me. "But I have absolutely felt the need to 'prove' that I was on the receiving end of a biased comment or discrimination and, in most cases, was met with 'Well, sorry that happened to you. Can't really help.'

"It really does come down to where you work," she explained, discussing whether there's a good way to encourage managers to be more fair about how they assign work or to at least be more proactive about bad behavior on their teams. "If you're in a psychologically safe environment where you can bring up these issues without repercussion, I could imagine that change could be made. But more often, managers get defensive or even want to protect themselves. That's why the onus to fix this should be on leaders and workplaces, not the marginalized."

Set and Protect Your Boundaries

(WORKING REMOTELY)

So much of what marginalized people go through at work comes down to the workplace environment: how people in the office get along with one another, who asks who out for coffee or for lunch, who gets along with whom, and so on. Unfortunately, even if you're objectively the most skilled and the most experienced person on your team, if you're being marginalized because of your race, your gender, or your disability status, there's nothing you can do to keep the cliquishness of that culture from seeping into your work and preventing you from doing your best. But in the early months of 2020, much of that changed. Many of us suddenly went from working in offices all the time and having to navigate the politics of being seen, being a superstar, and making a show of ourselves and our work around others to working at home, quietly, behind a screen, and only being seen by others for Zoom meetings and conference calls that were prescheduled. The COVID-19 pandemic threw a wrench into office cultures around the world, and some companies have permanently given up their office space. And other companies have used this moment to drastically rethink remote and hybrid work possibilities. The bright spot of this tragedy may be that there is a little more empathy for the worker. Or at least a little more flexibility.

There's a lot of good news here for marginalized workers like you or me. When I felt at my lowest at the *Times,* I rather enjoyed the flexibility of being able to do my work from home, listening to music if I chose to and using a computer that was far more powerful and flexible than the laptop I had been issued at work (and one with a way bigger screen). What's more, I had a more comfortable desk and chair and all the other personal touches I had already put into my workspace at home—something that many of my colleagues had to scramble to do when the pandemic set in and they were suddenly forced to set up home office spaces where none existed before. I enjoyed the peace and quiet, because here's the thing about being a marginalized person, even if you're going into the office: You feel that you need to be there to be seen—to be recognized as a member of the team or even as someone present, available, and willing to collaborate and help out on all the things you're being excluded from—but you also hate it. You hate being there, being seen, and going *just to be seen.* Those feelings come with a level of paranoia about what's going on behind your back when you're there *and* when you're not there, the meetings that could be happening right now but that you weren't invited to, and the anxiety of wondering how you're perceived when both you're there and when you're not.

Working remotely can alleviate this anxiety a bit. Not entirely, and it has its drawbacks, as we'll get into in a moment, but first let's discuss how you can use working remotely to your advantage. After all, when the currency of being present and being the loudest person in the room is diminished by the fact that everyone's remote, you have a unique opportunity to shine. And the same is true if you're on a hybrid-style team, where some people are in the office and others aren't. Hybrid-style teams can give rise to some misunderstandings and communication breakdowns, but there are definitely things you can do about it and moves you can make in silence to protect yourself and seek out that glamour work that you've been denied.

To get some tips, I turned to someone who's been working remotely much longer than I have. My friend and colleague Melanie Pinola is currently a writer at Wirecutter, the product review site owned by the *New York Times*. I've worked with Pinola in some form or fashion since both of us were writers at *Lifehacker*, and I was lucky enough to work with her again after she started at Wirecutter when I was its liaison to the newsroom. She's been working remotely for various employers since 1998, she told me. First, "as a telecommuter for a small marketing agency for over a dozen years, as a freelance writer working on remote teams like *Lifehacker* for five years, as part of the fully remote tech company Zapier for three years, and at Wirecutter for almost two years now. So, a long time."

Not that it takes more than twenty years of remote working experience to understand exactly how difficult it is to work remotely as a person of color or as a marginalized person in the workplace, but Pinola definitely has all the above. I asked her how she felt about remote work from a diversity perspective and whether she believed it was better or worse than in-person interaction and work. "I think remote work's emphasis on text-based communication (e.g., Slack and email) is great—no one is focusing on what I look or sound like, even though there are still clues, like my profile photo and my name," Pinola explained. "I feel less self-conscious, though, and more free to speak up, stripped of the physical cues to my age and race (and, if I changed my name, my gender)."

It's not all good news, though, she told me. After all, the social baggage that marginalized groups carry doesn't go away just because your colleagues can't see you all the time. Even if they only see you in Zoom meetings, it doesn't change their social conditioning (at best) or their prejudices (at worst). "It also depends on how the company and the people within it handle communicating remotely," Pinola continued. "In my experience, there are some managers who, after switching to remote or being unfamiliar with remote work, insist on having more video meetings and everyone having their cameras on during those meetings, negating those benefits. Also, if a company is only partially remote, it can be alienating for people who aren't in the office and aren't getting that face time that management seems to love—conversations and decisions happen in the office without them. That's not a diversity thing per se, but people with disabilities, who are juggling work with parenthood, who have many other reasons to want to work remotely, can be at a disadvantage if the culture isn't truly remote-friendly."

We'll explore that disconnect between working remotely and remote-work friendly companies shortly too, because people who have the option to work remotely and take it also have to deal with office cultures that don't always support the decision to work remotely. I continue to hope that the COVID-19 pandemic and the lessons we learn from it will smooth over those cracks and difficulties a bit, but we'll see. Even if the problems of remote work do improve somehow, the benefits will probably come to marginalized people last. So in the meantime, I'll talk about some things you can do to make sure you find success while you work remotely.

CHECK IN WITH PEOPLE YOU DON'T GET TO TALK TO

One of the benefits about working remotely—especially if everyone is doing it—is the opportunity to carve out time to talk to people you don't normally get to talk to. Without your conversation becoming fodder for the office rumor mill, that is. I remember once thinking to myself at a previous job, "Now's a great time to get familiar with some of the editors on some of the other teams!" So I sent out a few calendar appointments and emails inviting people to get coffee with me, and my action was startling enough that word of it actually came back around to some of the people who were actively marginalizing me. They, of course, told those same people whom I had invited to coffee that they shouldn't bother speaking to me. I remember that when I started my job at the *Times* and met all the wonderful section editors and leaders, one person—not particularly senior, but closer to my team than others—just told my manager, "I don't see why I should meet him," even though we'd be in meetings together for years after that. But working remotely means that there's a little less of that whispering behind your back. When you ask to meet someone, you can just send them an email or hop on a Zoom call, and if they go around you, trying to figure out what you want to talk about, you'll have a built-in understanding that this person probably isn't someone you'll actually want to work with.

So don't hesitate: Send a quick email to a colleague whom you'd love to work with but who is on another team, asking if they can spare fifteen minutes on a Zoom call just to catch up and discuss what both of you are working on and if there's anything you can do together. The benefit to everyone's being remote is that watercooler chat and office scuttlebutt are all replaced by video calls and off-to-the-side meetings like this, so you have a bit of a way in without having to force yourself into situations that you'd normally be uncomfortable in. If you're more comfortable with technology than some of your peers are, you can use that to your advantage as well. Besides, if you've been marginalized the way I have been, you wouldn't have been invited to those watercooler chats anyway. So now is a great time to see how you can work with other teams or on projects where you won't be marginalized or how you can take your big ideas to other people without the prying eyes of either jealous colleagues or an oppressive manager.

When I was feeling marginalized—in one job by management, and in another job by my peers—I realized that I actually had closer friends in different departments around the company than I had on my own team. Unfortunately, there was no real path for me to move to another team when things got bad. So instead, I focused on connecting with other team managers and peers to talk about how we could work together. Instead of trying to do the glamour work on my own team, I would try to come up with great new ideas and collaborations between my team (specifically, me) and their team—collaborations that we could highlight as examples of the great things we could do together. This approach was especially useful since I was able to collaborate with people who worked in different physical spaces or different offices even before we all started working remotely. It prepared me to collaborate with people via email, chat, video, and shared documents. Reach out to other people—those who may not be aware of what you're capable of and who are out of the reach of the people trying to keep your head down. Your bravery will usually be rewarded.

CONTROL THE WAY YOU WORK

In some ways, working remotely can help you be even more productive. You can carve out working time away from coworkers who buzz around your desk or demand your attention, and meetings are held virtually instead of in person. The problem with that always-on approach, though, is that it can be difficult to establish and maintain your professional boundaries when everyone's sitting around in front of their computers with no one to talk to. They'll reach out via email or Slack and interrupt what you're doing so they can chat. All it takes is one lonely colleague lighting up your direct messages or one overachiever sending emails in the middle of the night to turn what would normally be a relaxing evening into a stress-filled one— one where your phone won't stop alerting you about the work you hoped you'd left behind at the end of the day. That's why you need to protect your boundaries if you're going to work remotely for any length of time.

Many of us have struggled with setting boundaries for ages, and many of us have been campaigning for some level of work-life balance for just as long. On some level, this struggle exists mostly because if left to their own devices, most employers are perfectly fine letting you work all day and all night and won't enforce those boundaries for you. We wind up relying on the humanity and empathy of our managers to tell us to log off and go home, to stop checking email, to take our vacation days. It shouldn't have to be that way. So take a few simple steps.

Decide for yourself when you're at work and when you're off work. I wrote about this concept for *Wired*, but it's important for all of us to know when we're on and when we're off, and it needs to be something you're not trying to decide on the spot.[1] If it's 6:15 p.m. and you haven't already established that your day should end at 6 p.m., you're likely to just keep working until you feel like you're done. The problem is that this feeling seldom comes naturally—it comes with fatigue. If you must, clear those hours with your manager as well, just in case your boss is the type who wants to know for sure when you'll be around and when you won't. If you don't have to share this schedule with your boss, though, then don't—your hours can be things you observe without the watchful eye of the boss.

Turn off Slack, email, and other work-related notifications after a certain time of day. If you must, however, leave on notifications for anyone super important or from whom you'd want to hear after hours.

Set calendar reminders and blocked-off appointments for downtime. Be sure to schedule things like lunch, your morning coffee, an afternoon break, or anything else where you don't necessarily want to be disturbed. Set an appointment for your morning routine so people don't book a meeting with you earlier than you'd want, or schedule your own evening wrap-up so people don't try to force you into late meetings (you can always say, "Hey, I have an appointment, I have to run!").

Be clear in emails and other chats about when you'll get back to someone. If it's the end of the day and someone sends you a note, reply, letting them know you'll get to it tomorrow, just so the air is clear. Do the same for direct messages as well. Being clear up front will encourage people to respect your time—but it will also force others to be honest with you if they really do need you to take action before you stop for the day.

Don't be afraid to ask for comp time if you've been working late. This decision may vary from manager to manager, but your company should have in place a policy that says if you're working tons of overtime, you get some time back or off as a result. If you don't know what that policy is, ask. If you're a marginalized person in your workplace, it's just as possible that you don't know about it because no one wanted to tell you.

Set physical boundaries as well as mental and social ones. Give yourself a specific place where you settle in to work, and try to differentiate it from a place you use for relaxing or for play. If you're like me and use one computer for work and play, do something creative like changing the wallpaper when you're in work mode and changing it to something fun when you're off work. You can even download tools or set up a schedule so this change happens automatically. If you're lucky enough to have a home office that you can get up and leave at the end of the workday (and you don't need anything inside this office after working hours), do that. At the very least, make sure that at the end of the day, you get away from your computer or desk setup for a little while, just to relax and recalibrate before you sit back down to watch Netflix, browse Twitter, or play video games.

Once you've set these boundaries, the last and perhaps most important thing is to communicate them to the important people in your life. I'm not talking about your manager here—I'm talking about your spouse or partner, your children, and anyone who shares the same physical space with you. I also recommend telling your trusted colleagues, the ones who you know will respect you if you tell them not to ping you after hours unless it's urgent, about your boundaries. You never know, you may encourage others to do the same.

Now all of this sounds great . . . until you're the only Black person on your team and your boundaries are perceived as "aggressive" or "lazy." Or you're the Latinx person in the office and telling your colleagues that you're signing off at 6 p.m. every day makes you "fiery." Or you're the only woman in your group and telling colleagues that you have to take your lunch break every day gets a reaction like "Oh, need to take care of the kids?" Pick your battles, but push through these microaggressions (although, frankly, they're less "micro" than the term implies). Your boundaries are more important, and if there's anything you should spend some personal capital on at the office, it's making sure you're set up to do your best work *and* to care for your mental and emotional health.

MANAGE YOUR ENERGY, NOT YOUR TIME

And speaking of mental health, one of Pinola's best tips is to manage—and preserve—your mental energy, much as David Kadavy suggested. She said, "You and I have written a bunch about this before, but the best thing to do is manage your energy, not your time. Remote work—if it gives you scheduling flexibility—is great for that. Group related tasks together based on how much mental energy they require. Some people get a jolt after being in meetings, so you could time meetings when you're more likely to be sluggish (or vice versa, if meetings deplete your energy). But I think the number one thing is that people just want to be acknowledged and responded to as quickly as possible. I try to be as super clear as possible with my team and editors/managers where I am on a project (we use Basecamp for project management, but Slack updates are good, too). I don't think you can overcommunicate when it comes to keeping everyone in the loop."

SET UP YOUR SPACE FOR SUCCESS

In terms of physical boundaries, remote working works best when you have a physical space you actually enjoy working from. It should be someplace where you're comfortable having meetings and sitting for long periods, a place where you don't mind being on camera and where the tools that you need are within arm's reach. Not all of us have the privilege of a home office, but you can definitely do better than sitting on your couch with all your work papers spread out over the coffee table (unless, of course, that's your personal vibe).

KEEP YOUR SPACE ORGANIZED

But remember, if you're subject to additional scrutiny because you're part of a minority community, then you have to take extra precautions with your home workspace. Unlike your privileged colleagues, before you jump on camera for a meeting, you need to make sure the space behind you on camera is especially clean and tidy. I not only keep the space behind me organized to a certain extent, but I also like to keep a few objects of interest that people can home in on and ask me about if they're curious—it's one way to diffuse any potential tension. If you have to use the company laptop to do your work, be sure you make room for it on your desk, so you can switch between that and your personal computer if you like. I'm a big fan of using multiple monitors connected to one computer so that various open tools can be displayed at once, and the best monitors even let you connect multiple computers and switch between them based on the one you need to use. That way I'm not hunched over the company laptop day in and day out—I can connect it to the thirty-four-inch monitors that are at the core of my desk setup. (You don't have to go as hard as I did here, though. I am a tech journalist, after all.)

And even if you're not a tech journalist, invest in the workspace elements that you use the most. Sure, you may want a shiny new keyboard and mouse, and those things are fine, believe me, but consider how many hours a day you spend in your desk chair. Now multiply that by the number of days you sit at your desk per week. Now multiply that by the number of weeks you plan to work remotely this year. Adds up quickly, doesn't it? As my former colleague Jason Chen, who used to write and edit for *Gizmodo* and *Lifehacker* and who now runs StoryBundle, a site where you can buy e-books in themed batches, said, "Spend your money where your time is."[2] Like your bed, where you spend over 40 percent of your life, your desk chair is probably the object you use the most in your workspace. Invest in a good one. You don't necessarily have to spend thousands on a high-end Herman Miller chair if you don't want to. Search the used office-furniture market; you can often find ergonomically designed office chairs for a fraction of their retail prices. Even so-called gaming chairs are coming along in terms of ergonomics and are worth a look. Either way, don't just sit on a wooden dining room chair with a pillow on it. You can do better, and your back and posture will thank you.

And don't overlook any workplace benefits or perks you may be offered to customize your home workspace. Maybe your company offers a small stipend for office equipment. Ask your company's

HR department if it does, or if it will pay for a new monitor or office chair so that you can work from home more comfortably. Maybe your company, like my employer, even offers a home fitness stipend in lieu of gym memberships so you can get a little exercise as well.

MAKE SURE YOU AND YOUR MANAGER ARE ALWAYS ON THE SAME PAGE

Regardless of whether you and your manager get along, working remotely will strain your relationship with this individual. It's natural—times when they would be more inclined to just stop by and see how you're doing now have to be planned. If you worked near each other, your boss can no longer just stand up and see that you're busy with a task. Not every manager is paranoid that the employees aren't working if they're not being watched, but almost every supervisor would appreciate a check-in from time to time. So use remote work as an opportunity to connect with your boss a little more closely. You may find that the communication you develop while you're all working from home will continue when you're back in the office.

Once you've settled in working remotely, whether it's by choice or because everyone is doing it, ask your manager for regular one-on-ones. You two can decide how often they should be, but I'd suggest starting with weekly and then skipping here and there if there's nothing to discuss or if something more pressing is going on. A half-hour is probably enough, as Kathi Elster and Katherine Crowley, authors of *Working with You Is Killing Me*, explained earlier. You just have to make sure those meetings actually happen rather than getting bumped or canceled because your manager might think there's nothing to discuss.

Pinola agrees. She said that one of the benefits of remote work in this case is that you have the time and flexibility to make sure you're as communicative and clear as possible. "Because most of the conversation happens in text [or chat or email]," she explained, "you have more time to reflect on your work before you have to share project progress. For example, instead of running into your boss in the hallway and being asked for a status update, you have time in Slack or whatever to give a thoughtful answer. For people who are marginalized at work and aren't always front and center at meetings, I think remote communication is a boon. I personally feel more comfortable saying things in writing/text than I do when speaking—and I imagine other people who have non-US/English accents or voices and faces that aren't well represented would feel the same."

Don't let your manager steer the conversation unless they are a particularly good boss and know what they want out of a one-on-one. Remember, as Crowley and Elster told me, most managers aren't taught how to manage people—they get promoted because they're good at a thing, so the company assumes they must be good at managing other people who do the thing. So put together a quick agenda for yourself for things that you'd like to cover with your boss: projects you're working on, tasks on your plate, your priorities, and so on. For those of you pressured into doing the office housework or the other tasks that we're expected to do but that leave us marginalized, now is a good time to update your manager on the projects you wish you were working on or the ideas you'd love to bring to life. It's also a great opportunity to fill out your work diary and bring your manager in on the things you've been documenting. This all serves two purposes: It makes sure your manager never has to wonder exactly what you're up to, should someone else ask them, and it makes sure your manager knows they can trust you to manage your priorities.

It's difficult to overstate the importance of communicating with your boss. Nothing reinforces marginalization at work like being out of touch with your supervisor. Such a communication gap is revealed in a manager's "Hell if I know" when someone asks them what you're responsible for on their team. Or even worse is the answer "I'm not sure. I haven't spoken to them in a while." Remote work may feel like an opportunity to be free of the leash of your manager, and on some level it certainly is, but that freedom comes with a responsibility to show your manager that you really deserve it. Sure, you shouldn't have to prove you're working hard, and depending on your manager, you may not need to. But for most of us, our bosses want us to keep in touch. And even if that's not the case for you, it can't hurt to make sure you check in.

DOCUMENT YOUR WORK

Although I've touched on the value of bringing your manager in on your work diary, working remotely makes it even more important to document everything you're working on. You don't need to log every minute of every day, but you should always have a quick list of what you're doing, where you're at in a project you're seeing through, or just a checklist of what you plan to work on next. Even if you and your manager are on the same page (and odds are, even if you are, they'll still forget), other people in your office may come asking what you have going on because they want your help. When you reach out to other teams to see how you can collaborate, you need to know if you have the bandwidth to do the thing you're proposing. And when you do take on new work, you need to have a place where you can note what it is and what level of effort it requires.

On one level, this documentation is for others—so you can quickly react if anyone questions your worth or value to the team or organization. On the other level, a work diary is for you. This way, being physically disconnected from your colleagues doesn't mean having to feel disconnected from the work you're doing. As discussed earlier, a weekly review or running tally of your work means that you'll always be aware of what you're doing and what kind of work it is (glamour work or housework, work that will advance your career or busywork assigned to you for other reasons). The review will also give you fodder to update your résumé or brag a little about your own successes to others in your industry. And of course, because so many of us have been working remotely during the COVID-19 pandemic, when we do start to go back into offices full time, you'll have a ready-made answer to questions like "So, what did you do over the pandemic?"

WORKING REMOTELY
CAN ALSO FURTHER ALIENATE YOU

Now here's the flip side of the remote-work coin: Everyone likes the idea of working remotely when we can stop doing so whenever we want to and go back into the office. However, if it's *not* a requirement, working remotely can also further marginalize or alienate you from the rest of your team who may be in the office at any given moment while you're sitting at home wondering why no one is replying to your messages on Slack or the emails you sent that morning. It could mean missing out on impromptu meetings and other not-quite-formal events where people toss around ideas or even collaborate on projects—projects that you've already been marginalized from, so no one is going to speak up and say, "Hey, we should get so-and-so's opinion on this." That's the frustrating side of remote work: In some ways, as it was for me at the *Times*, it can be a deadly cycle. You start to dread being in the office because you're marginalized, so you continue the marginalization by physically removing yourself from the space and working alone, remotely, at home, with only chat, video calls, and emails as your bridge to everything going on in your absence.

That's why if you have a hybrid team, it can be even more important to periodically head into the office to make sure you get some face time with people, as irritating as it may be, just to be seen. It's why these tips are even more important when you have to use tools to virtually shorten the physical distance between you and your colleagues. You have to be even more proactive about seeking out those office relationships and working around any other cliques that may form when you're not involved. Also, avoid taking small slights personally, even if they are intended personally. Not everyone who leaves you off a calendar appointment is trying to reinforce the marginalization you're feeling, and not everyone who forgets to cc you on that email chain thinks you're untalented or lazy or too brassy to work with. Another approach would be to spend time and energy trying to figure out the offender's intentions, as suggested in the discussion of microaggressions. Or you could just move on, while quietly waiting to see if the person becomes a repeat offender or just made an honest mistake. Keep plugging away, doing the work you know how to do best, and ideally working around anyone who's actively trying to keep you out of the conversation.

Being good at working in an office environment doesn't necessarily translate to being good at remote work, after all. "I have definitely become more hermit-like because I've worked full time from home for decades now," Pinola told me. "Before COVID, I did have to go into Wirecutter's Long Island City office a few times to test products, and it was a strange experience. I felt like I was a visitor at the office, rather than someone who belonged there, but that's largely because I never went into the office. I tried to use those times when I went in (because going into the office takes about an hour and a half each way commuting) to reconnect with some of my teammates, and I always enjoyed it, even though I wouldn't have wanted to do that every day." If, like me, you consider the notion of getting face time stressful, especially when you could just contentedly be working from home, where you have a routine and you're comfortable, then consider making it something you do semiregularly so you can mentally prepare for it.

"I'm really just an introvert, though, who likes people," Pinola told me—and I grinned because I'm exactly the same. "So on any given day, depending on how much social interaction I've had, I may or may not want to go out for coffee. I think you can have office-politics-y skills like schmoozing even if you're typically a remote worker-slash-hermit, because online chat now can do fairly the same amount of things, minus physical high-fiving. And you can have or sharpen those skills outside of work." So don't feel too bad about having Zoom coffees instead of coffee meetings, or Slack chats instead of full one-on-ones if meeting in person gives you anxiety (or even if it gives you anxiety because you normally are never in the office).

"Probably the most important skill I've learned (but perhaps not mastered) is communicating without too much irony or sarcasm," Pinola said. "I'm naturally a sarcastic person, but often that doesn't come across as I intend, because text doesn't carry the same inflections and weight on words. So, after many face-palming interactions—in email, tweets, Slack, et cetera—I'm super careful now to make sure that what I write is clear if it's a joke or something tongue-in-cheek. I recommend liberal emoji usage."

RULE 14

Data Is Power,
and Power Is Money

(GETTING PAID)

N one of us goes to work just because we feel like it; we go to pay the bills, finance our lives, and save for our futures. And whether we want to acknowledge it or not, there is also plenty of self-worth tied in with our wages. That's why it's so important to make sure you're paid right, no matter what you do for a living. Again, I'm not here to prove that minority and marginalized groups earn less than their privileged colleagues do and that marginalized people are systemically disadvantaged when it comes to accumulating and retaining wealth. There's no shortage of data that shows exactly how poorly paid women and people of color are compared with their white and male colleagues, not just in the United States, but across the globe.[1] As just one example, for every dollar a man makes in America, a woman earns eighty-two cents, according to the U.S. Labor Department.[2] And when you add ethnicity to the equation, the numbers get worse. For every dollar that a white man makes, a Black man makes eighty-eight cents. Black women, on the other hand, instead of earning eighty-two cents like their white female peers do, make seventy-six cents. Some of those differences have to do with job types, but when controlled for education, location, and experience, the disparity stands, according to PayScale, a tech company that compiles compensation data.[3] The real question is, How do you make sure that you're being paid appropriately for your experience, skills, and in comparison with your colleagues?

For those without privilege, the cards are stacked against you. As Kristin Wong, journalist and author of *Get Money*, a book all about making sure you get paid what you're worth, so aptly puts it, "In an ideal world, you'd be able to bring up your concerns without being penalized, but in an ideal world, you wouldn't be underpaid in the first place."

The first step to getting paid appropriately is to figure out exactly how much you're worth, a difficult-enough task if you don't trust your manager or company to give you an honest answer. Often, HR departments say their salaries are "competitive" and "industry standard," but there's no reason for you to take their word for it.

Plus, so much of our collective office culture thrives on the secrecy around salaries and the taboo on people's sharing how much they make, especially in comparison with their peers at the same company or even across entire industries. If your company doesn't have a policy stating outright that employees can't discuss their salaries or benefits with each other, then I'm willing to bet that they at least discourage it. I've only worked at one company that *didn't* discourage us from sharing our salaries if we wanted to, but the firm didn't explicitly encourage it, either. Even the *New York Times*, where our reporters would actively investigate and cover labor issues like pay inequality and discrimination in the workplace, discussing our salaries with each other certainly wasn't encouraged. And if pay disparities were uncovered, usually an array of excuses and justifications came out to explain why a white male editor made dozens of thousands of dollars more than did their black female colleague who had more experience. A former colleague who penned an entire article about how important it was to be fearless about sharing your salary with your coworkers to make sure you're being paid fairly never, ever—not once!—shared his salary with me to make sure *we* were being paid fairly. And when I began to bring it up, he ducked the issue.

"Data is power, and power is money, so if you want more money, you need both data and power," said Emma Carew Grovum, founder of Kimbap Media and a journalism consultant who helps media organizations correct structural issues of inequality in their workplaces. "Data comes from having those tough conversations with your friends and colleagues, not just in your own organization but across your industry. I tweet my salary history several times per year, because I think it's important to raise awareness among young BIPOC [Black, Indigenous, and People of Color] folks." Even then, she explained, data may not be enough: "I was fortunate enough to have a good boss at my final internship, who offered to tell me whether my first job salary was a strong offer or not. It wasn't, and he encouraged me to negotiate, which I did, but was unsuccessful. The advice that he gave me was to always negotiate, even if they stand their ground, even if you aren't successful, because it's important for the company and your manager to understand how you value yourself."

FIRST, FIND OUT HOW MUCH YOU'RE WORTH

Before you can get paid appropriately, you have to know what your skills and experience are worth. That's tough, because part of it has to do with communicating with others in your industry or in your exact position to find out how much they make. But before you do that, it helps to do a little digging as though you were applying for your own job for the first time. Websites like Glassdoor, Salary .com, PayScale, and LinkedIn are all designed to help you figure out what people who do what you do in your field make, depending on where they live.

- **Glassdoor:** With Glassdoor, you can search specific companies and roles to find out more about them and search specific roles in your city or region to find out how much those companies pay. Even better, Glassdoor acts as a bit of a repository for company reviews, so you can get an idea of what people who worked at the company think of it. Just take the reviews with the same grain of salt you take product reviews when you shop online. It's natural that people who are more disgruntled will leave more reviews in the first place, and overly glowing reviews are equally suspect. If you see recurring themes, make note, but if you're looking for future opportunities and want to make sure you're being paid appropriately, it's a great place to look.

- **Salary.com:** After giving Salary.com your job title and city, it will generate a chart and give you a national average salary for that role (or the closest job it can find to the one you entered), along with outliers so that you can see how you compare with the industry average. If the service has data for more senior or more junior roles, it will offer that as well. You can also add things like your education level and years of experience to see if these factors change anything.

- **PayScale:** This software company offers similar features to Glassdoor and Salary.com, along with a wealth of information about the pay gap between male and female employees and between white and minority employees across industries. If you still doubt whether the gender or racial pay gap exists, PayScale has the data to make it crystal clear for you. You can search salary information at PayScale not just by job or industry but also by degree or certification, so you can decide whether going back to school or paying for a certification exam or course will pay for itself in the future.

- **LinkedIn:** While it's not a repository of salaries, LinkedIn is a great place to connect with other people in your industry and to discuss how much they're making and how much other companies pay their staff. On this platform, you can also read other people's writing on salary transparency and equity and even find some like-minded discussion groups to join. Plus, as you meet people through LinkedIn and see job openings that have their salaries listed, you'll get a feeling for how much your skills and qualifications are worth and what big or small things you could do to stand out from your peers and increase your earning potential.

Using the internet is certainly one way to figure out what you should be making, but it's not perfect, and it's not universal. You're relying on a lot of other people to collect the information, organize it, and make sure that it's accurate. And while no doubt the sites I mentioned do their best in this regard, sometimes there's no excuse for simply talking to people about salaries. But that's where the problems arise.

WATCH YOUR BACK

The salary transparency discussion often leaves minority and marginalized people behind. There are risks to asking and talking about transparency and equity either from management or HR, or additional marginalization from colleagues.

And that doesn't even speak to how difficult it can feel, when you are marginalized, to even approach your privileged colleagues, the ones getting the glamour work while you're stuck with the office housework, and just strike up a conversation on the importance of equality and fairness. I'm willing to bet that it's not necessarily a topic they'd be horribly interested in being forthcoming about, especially to someone they're actively pushing to the side.

There are a few ways to get around this, but first you should be absolutely aware of the risks. If the hammer comes down from HR because you and your peers are having salary conversations, or if your manager learns that you've found out your colleague makes more than you do for the same job and experience level, the consequences will almost certainly be harsher for you. Marginalized workers, especially workers of color, get caught in a kind of punishment loop where they're disciplined for infractions others wouldn't be. They're then judged more harshly in performance reviews for those same infractions, and this disparity then has deeper, longer-lasting effects on their careers. Because marginalized workers are more likely to be overlooked for promotions, fired outright, or laid off over those so-called performance issues, it is more difficult for them to get future jobs. I've experienced this sort of discrimination firsthand, and you probably have as well. Just be careful before you charge into this topic. The stakes and repercussions are higher for you than they are for others.

"The argument for transparency is that it's harder for employers to hide behind unconscious bias when salaries are made transparent," Wong said, "but research doesn't always support that idea. There's research out of UCLA that found wage transparency oddly reinforces inequality because it benefits higher-paying workers just as much as it benefits their lower-paid counterparts. And maybe because transparency is positioned as a cure-all to pay inequality, we accept it as a solution before there's actually progress."[4]

DO YOUR RESEARCH IN SAFE SPACES

With that warning out of the way, I'm still going to tell you to ask around about salaries. Why? It's the only way to get real, firsthand data. The key is to talk to the right people, in the right spaces, if you have access to these people. "The more like-minded people you can pull into your network, the better," said Wong. "You might not be able to get much support from your direct coworkers, but maybe there are colleagues in other departments you can connect with. Or maybe there are affinity groups within your industry that you can join."

We discussed affinity groups, sometimes called employee resource groups, earlier. They're often centered around identity, sexuality, disability, or some other common interest, like the Black@ NYT group that I joined at the *Times*. If you have access to ERGs at your company, they're a good place to start asking about salaries and fair compensation if you have the psychological safety to do it. "These groups can be especially useful communities for minority workers who feel like outsiders in the workplace," Wong continued. "You can share important issues, get social support and advice, and even devise a plan of action for those issues. If you're looking for an affinity group to join, LinkedIn or Facebook can be a good place to start. But you could even start your own affinity group by organizing with a few like-minded colleagues or peers you trust."

Taking the conversation to a broader industry level is an excellent suggestion. When I was a project manager, I could go to local chapter meetings or networking events held by the Project Management Institute and talk with other people in my field. There I could hear not only about fair pay, but also about what other companies paid their project managers and which industries were growing and needed people with my skills. Even now, I'm a member of the National Association of Black Journalists, which often hosts panels and sessions on issues of pay inequality in our industry. These sessions are designed to remind me how much my skills are worth and to make sure I don't settle for employers who will pay me less.

Unions are also an ally. The past several years have seen a number of high-profile unionizations and union drives, from journalists organizing their newspapers or magazines to Amazon warehouse workers leading the charge for fair pay and sick days. Union organizing is no small feat, to be sure, but if you have a union in your field, part of its mission is to make sure that its members are paid fairly by their employers. And even if you're not a member, organizers and other members are likely more than happy to share information on pay rates in the industry so that you can earn what you're worth. "Union contracts can be another way to find information about compensation for your role, even if your company isn't union-ized," Carew Grovum said. "Again, the more data points you have will help bolster your case. Ideally, you would have firsthand infor-mation from your colleagues. If you can't get that, find out what folks make in your industry in similar companies. Even better, find out what folks make at your top competitors."

Carew Grovum offered several other suggestions to help you un-cover industry salaries, depending on where you work. "Another way to find out what your (probably white) colleagues are making, if you happen to work at a nonprofit, is to search your organization's IRS 990 Form. Nonprofits are required to report their top earners' salaries above a certain threshold," she explained.

"Finally," she said, "if you work in a public organization such as a city government or a state university, there is a good chance that your department's salaries are public records and can therefore be requested under a Freedom of Information Act request in your state. This obviously varies by state and institution." Remember, you don't have to be a journalist or have the backing of some media organiza-tion to file a FOIA request, either. Anyone can.

If you're reading this and thinking that your industry doesn't have organizations like that, consider rallying some people to your side and starting your own organization, even if it's local to your city or community. Sometimes it can just start with a few posts on social media looking for others in your field to talk to or starting a group on Facebook or LinkedIn to share your challenges and in-viting others to share their experiences. This capability—to start a professional group—is one in which LinkedIn shines. A num-ber of people—especially early-career professionals—generally see LinkedIn as emblematic of the bad kind of networking, full of po-lite smiles and forced handshakes. And while it can certainly be that, if you spend a little more time on the service, you can find some people genuinely interested in connecting with others in their industry, and you can find plenty of discussion groups and forums dedicated to your industry, whatever that may be.

Use the internet to your benefit here: You can get better, real-time advice from others in your industry as long as you're willing to potentially wade through the opinions of others in the process. Just be careful you don't put too much of yourself out there in your quest to just learn more about your field. Opening up in public, especially on social media, carries risks of harassment and toxicity, so treat it like you were at a cocktail party talking to people you don't *quite* know that well. Protect yourself but ask openly and honestly and take the responses you get with appropriate skepticism. And if you get the feeling that someone is trying to engage with you in bad faith, then do yourself a favor and don't engage at all.

NEGOTIATION IS NOT A PANACEA; IT'S A START

Before we go wholesale into the topic of salary negotiation, Wong offered a stark reminder that negotiating your salary can go more than one way. "Traditional personal finance advises workers to simply bring up issues to a manager and negotiate a raise. But we all know in the real world it's not that easy. A 2018 study published in the *Journal of Applied Psychology* found that Black workers get paid *less* when they negotiate salary, for example. You have to tread carefully," she told me.[5]

Even so, data is your best friend and really the only weapon you have. Especially if you plan to go into a conversation with your employer about pay disparities between you and your colleagues or between your role and the same role at other companies. You need to make sure you pull that information together in a concrete, comprehensive way before you go into your boss's office, guns blazing, asking for a raise or threatening to quit for another opportunity.

"If you find out you're being underpaid, I'm not sure it's wise to outrightly tell your boss you've been talking to coworkers and believe you're being compensated unfairly," Wong said. "Even though it may be true, and even though there are laws that protect you from being punished for talking openly about salary with colleagues, that punishment usually happens covertly and subtly in workplaces. Your best course of action—and one I've used myself—is to gather research to support your case for a higher salary. Research similar jobs and job descriptions on LinkedIn or Glassdoor to see what other workers in similar roles are earning. Quantify your own wins and accomplishments in the workplace. Focus the negotiation around the data as much as you can."

Carew Grovum agreed. "Sometimes it is as simple as approaching your manager and revealing the [salary] discrepancy," she said. "I once negotiated a raise for myself by bringing a job posting from a competitor to my boss. The company was a union shop and therefore posted salary bands for their jobs. In this particular instance, a similar but smaller role than the one I was playing was offering a minimum of thirty thousand dollars more than I made at the time. I made this point to my boss, in addition to handing him a massive amount of evidence. It painted a stark picture for my boss: me interviewing for this other job. And my salary was increased by almost forty percent."

EXPAND YOUR ZONE OF POSSIBILITY

As mentioned earlier, I once worked for a CIO who was very demanding but from whom I learned a great deal. The concept of the *zone of possibility* was one of the things I learned from him. I'm sure he didn't invent the concept, but in 2015, Patti Phillips, CEO of Women Leaders in College Sports, gave a TED talk that focused on the same idea.[6] Basically, when you think about negotiation, your zone of possibility is often restrained by what you, personally, think is possible in that situation. Unfortunately, those limitations are often self-imposed and don't reflect what the other person has the power to offer you or would even like to offer you if you asked. The CIO demonstrated the full weight of the zone of possibility when he would negotiate with technology services vendors. He asked them to lower the price not only for the equipment our company needed to buy but also for things like training courses for the staff, ongoing support, on-site help, on-call technicians, and other things that huge tech companies are more than happy to offer their customers. Where others thought they were sitting down to talk prices only, he was there to talk about far more than that.

That's something I keep with me to this day: When you negotiate salary, you're not just negotiating dollars. You can also, if you wish, negotiate benefits, additional vacation or sick time, office equipment like a new laptop or smartphone, and more. Carew Grovum offered a few more compensation ideas when we talked about it. "Everything is negotiable and on the table. Start thinking about your salary as just part of a total compensation package," she said. She suggested negotiating for more money but in different forms, such as one-time bonuses, retention bonuses, and annual bonuses.

Dues to professional organizations and industry groups are also costs that your company may be willing to shoulder if it can't give you a bigger raise. You may even be able to get things like money for workshops, certifications that will boost your career potential, tuition reimbursement, or even your monthly cell phone bill or home internet if you work on the go. Consider asking for things like a transit stipend or reimbursement if your company doesn't already offer one—and if they do, ask for the firm to take on more of the weight or something like a bigger 401(k) match. Even better, Carew Grovum suggested, ask for more flex time, like the ability to work your own best hours or work from home more frequently. You could also ask to go remote most days and come to the office only when you're needed for meetings and such.

One of my former *Times* colleagues, after she negotiated a better job and left the paper, now works for a fully remote company. She moved out of the expensive New York City metro area to a smaller, more affordable community. Instead of insisting that she live close to an office, the new company said it was fine and let her keep her NYC salary while living in a suburb close enough to drive in when she needed to be in the office but far enough away that the cost of living is more affordable. She couldn't be happier (and frankly, I'm kind of jealous).

So before you go in thinking that the only good result from a salary negotiation is more money, consider asking for all those other things that may make your life easier or make you even more valuable both to your current employer and to future ones.

USE DATA TO MAKE YOUR BEST CASE

Knowing your worth is half the battle. You also have to have a clear plan for presenting the information. "I wanted a big promotion once, so I started bringing my boss pieces of evidence, bit by bit," Carew Grovum said. "First, I gave him some reading, a few industry publication articles about why the position I was advocating for was on the rise. I even remember highlighting key passages, in case he was too busy to read the entire thing. Next, I brought him a job description I had written for myself. It included what my expanded duties would look like. It also included a new hire for my newly created team and went on to explain which of my current duties I could delegate to this person. Later I added a 'goals for my team next year' and a 'budget' document. I didn't get exactly what I wanted, but I did get a new title and an intern to run a pilot project. More importantly, I had shown him how big my vision was, and we were able to find a compromise that put me on that pathway."

The conversation you have with your manager is important. Managers reward ambition and a go-getter attitude, but marginalized employees have to walk the line between being seen as ambitious and greedy in a way their white, majority coworkers don't. Bringing up your career goals and the ideas you'd love to work on— if only you had the right resources, of course—on a regular basis will help them remember that you have the same drive as your other colleagues without running the risk of coming off as someone who only has big ideas when it's time to get a raise. Some people can get away with that, but frankly? We can't.

Your regular one-on-one meetings with your manager are a great time to seed your goals and achievements the way that Carew

Grovum suggested. Let your boss know you see the great things other people in your company are doing, and you'd like to be involved. Discuss your big ideas and your small ones. Describe—and quantify—how much more you could do if you had a team of people reporting to you. Your manager may balk at that, but you've at least planted the seed in their minds that you're thinking about the future, particularly your future with the company. Then, suggest a smaller, more manageable project that you'd enjoy running, even if you ran it yourself. Quantify that as well, in terms of things that matter to your boss: sales, readers, subscriptions, new clients, whatever your metrics might be. You may get those opportunities without having to campaign for them in one big meeting where you ask for a raise, but even if you don't, you've already proven you're both career-minded and ambitious. And even if your boss never appreciates these qualities, they are skills that will prove valuable in interviews and in other jobs.

At some point, you just have to do it—you have to go in and ask for more than you're getting now. And here, your work diary is a huge asset when it comes to asking for a raise. It's your personal data. The point of keeping it, in addition to helping you navigate the day-to-day and offer some catharsis, is to keep track of why you're doing the work you do and to note your successes, big or small. Those are the types of things you want to bring up when you meet with a manager to discuss all the value you bring to their team and to the company. "When you score big," Carew Grovum said, "when you have a win or a success (even small ones), make sure you document them. Screenshot and save those emails with high praise from on high. This helps you tell the story of your own success, which is key to negotiating for a higher salary." She also reasserted how important it is to have regular one-on-one meetings where you can regularly remind your manager exactly what you're doing so they are not surprised when you come in asking for a raise.

THE COUNTEROFFER

If you've already done your digging and, hopefully, have an idea of how much others in your role at your company are paid, then you know how much people who do your job elsewhere in the industry make. Your company or manager may claim that the situation is different for those other companies and that they don't have the budget to offer you a raise. But if you start contacting those other companies about their open jobs and pull in an offer from one of them, your boss or your company will most likely find the budget to give you a counteroffer pretty quickly. And if they don't, well, you're free to move on to something new with a higher salary or better benefits.

But sometimes, especially if you are marginalized, your manager—or HR—may not take kindly to your even bringing an outside offer in the first place. "Some employers don't react well to folks bringing an outside offer to the table as leverage," Carew Grovum said. "So do your research on how this tactic has worked for others in the recent past. I've had it work for me, but I've seen it backfire for others. The first (really only) time I pulled it off, my boss told me it was fine and it worked out, but that I hadn't played my cards well at all. Preferences on this practice really vary from manager to manager and company to company. I've known folks who worked in shops where the *only* way to get a raise was to go get an outside offer and bring it back to the table. So it totally depends on where you are and what the culture is." Carew Grovum also gave the same warning I mentioned earlier: "Just because it worked for your white colleague, do not assume it will work for your BIPOC self. Further, just because your boss tells you it's cool and that they would 'totally understand' if you are seeking other offers and that you should feel comfortable telling them about where you are at in other searches doesn't mean it's in *your* best interest to do so. Don't come to the table with an offer you aren't willing to actually take."

Carew Grovum's last piece of advice is extremely important. I've been in roles where I wanted to make more than I was making. After scouting around, doing some interviewing, applying to other jobs, and eventually landing an offer for more than I was currently making, I went to my manager to let them know that another company had offered me more. I laid out all the things that I did for my boss and the company and asked if they could do anything about the discrepancy. My manager smiled, shook my hand, wished me luck at my new job, promised to throw a potluck going-away party before my last day, and then asked me when that last day would be. Even worse, some coworkers in places I've worked said that trying to leverage a better job offer may work to get a raise in the short term, but they eventually found themselves even more marginalized than they were before they asked. Their manager and colleagues—now aware of the raise and the external job offer—gave them the cold shoulder. In one case, one manager openly, in discussions with fellow managers, used the fact that they had recently given someone a raise to correct a huge salary discrepancy on his team as an excuse not to give him an annual increase that year. And, you guessed it, the decision just created a new discrepancy between the employee and the rest of the team.

"A mentor once told me it's a bad idea to leverage an outside job offer, then stay at the same company, because your employee then knows they may need to replace you in the future," Wong told me. "You immediately make yourself dispensable, this mentor argued. That's one way of looking at it, but different employers will respond differently. I once interviewed an HR professional who told me the most effective way to increase your salary is to leverage job offers, and I tend to agree. When you negotiate, you need evidence to back up your ask, and what better evidence than an actual salary offer you can point to? On the other hand, if you're leveraging the offer at a company that doesn't value you in the first place, it might be better to take a chance on the new role that's offering you a higher salary from the start. It highly depends on the situation—there are no hard-and-fast rules to navigate workplace discrimination. In most cases, you have to use your own judgment."

When you go out to get that external job offer, practice singing your own praises the way you would to your current manager. Let the prospective employers know all about the great things you're currently working on and share some of those same wins from your work diary. That's what it's there for! Similarly, don't tell them what you make now—tell them what you want to make, in light of the research you've already done on similar positions in the industry, "especially if you are or have been underpaid," Carew Grovum said. "Instead, remind them that it's actively illegal to require this in some states (like New York). If that doesn't work, remind them that this is a tactic that has historically been used to keep women and people of color underpaid, and they don't want to reinforce a bad stereotype, now would they?"

RULE 15

Your Job Is Not Your Friend

(KNOWING WHEN TO GO)

At the *Times,* I never really felt like I had a place, because I was so often excluded. As time progressed and the team dynamics changed, some people left the team, and others were pulled away to work on more-high-profile projects, and I felt more and more isolated. So I was in a position that I thought was prestigious, but I didn't have the opportunity to work with people I enjoyed working with. I even felt stymied when trying to do work that I loved and thought would be powerful. In some cases, I even felt unwelcome and unwanted (and, to be honest, I sometimes was). I was depressed and found myself working remotely for no reason other than the fact that I could. People wouldn't notice my absence. I'd go into the office from time to time for meetings, interviews, events, and other opportunities to pick up interesting work, but otherwise when I was in the office, I'd often stay quiet at my desk, keeping to myself and churning out the office housework that kept the team alive and our metrics high enough to clearly show that we were doing great work. But at the end of every day I was there, I would leave the office the same way I came in: by exchanging more words with the security guards—also people of color—who worked at the front desk than I often did with anyone I saw in the office itself.

Part of my professional solitude had to do with my own social anxiety, combined with being actively marginalized. It's difficult to set up coffee meetings and other one-on-ones with colleagues you'd like to work with when, first, everyone's busy and you already feel as if you're imposing just by asking for some of their time and, second, you've been made to feel awful about your very presence in the space, as though you somehow don't deserve to be there. Putting both of those things together made me even more reluctant to dream up big ideas (because I didn't know who would work with me on them, and sharing them with people I didn't already trust meant potentially losing them to someone who'd claim them for themselves) and try to do new things. Instead, I kept my head down and just churned out work that I was proud of and that had great impact but was 100 percent "in my lane."

HOW TO MAKE CHANGE

For me, change was about three steps. Making the time to start going to Black@NYT events and meetings was the first step. It was a small thing, because they were lightly attended and often the people there knew each other already, so again, I was an outsider. But I was welcome, and that was all the difference. Even when I was nervous to speak, people received my ideas thoughtfully. Even when I felt out of place, people appreciated my presence. It was, for the first time, a space where I felt welcomed outside of specific meetings with some editors who I knew were glad to have me but whom I didn't get to work with regularly. Joining that community of journalists of color went a long way as well and reminded me that I—and my experiences—were valid.

The second step was therapy. I know it's not an option for everyone, either because of lack of access or because of just straight-up affordability (and trust me, I know how expensive therapy can be, but I paid for it anyway). And I know that in some communities, therapy is still a stigmatizing discussion. But having a truly objective person—someone with no strings attached to my life or my career—can be incredibly helpful. I could open up to this person about how horrible that one coworker was, and how he regularly made me so angry my partner took me to New York City's Rage Cage (you pay a few dollars for an hour to work out your anger on a box of breakable objects with a variety of blunt objects) for my birthday. To this date, it was still one of the best presents I've ever received. But a rage room doesn't help you build positive coping mechanisms.

Talking to a therapist—one who really understands your life and your specific struggles—does, and it was transformative for me. The therapist helped me brainstorm ways I could stand up for myself in the workplace—ways that were true to my personality—while still being honest and assertive. He helped me find the line between being fearful of social judgment because of my Blackness in predominantly white spaces and being proud of my accomplishments and truthful about my needs (I'm still working on that).

Whatever spaces you may need to navigate, whether it's male-dominated spaces and you're a woman, or queer-unfriendly spaces and you're a member of the LGBTQ+ community, or inaccessible spaces and you're disabled, having someone who has no ties to what you're dealing with but with whom you can openly share your thoughts and feelings is a lifesaver, quite literally.

And here's another tip related to therapy: Don't lie to your therapist or sidestep difficult conversations. It can be tempting, and my therapist has had to call me out several times when I'm clearly bending the truth or straight-out lying to pretend that I'm making more progress than I am, or because I want him to like me instead of treat me. Therapy is expensive, and sessions are only on average an hour long (usually less). Spend your time and money wisely, and let the therapist help you.

The third step was finding a community of people who welcomed me for who I was and who encouraged me to share my experiences the way they shared their own. A community where we could hear each other's voices and lift each other up in a way I honestly hadn't seen before. For me, that was joining the Journalists of Color group, a community of journalists around the globe, all talking to each other using Slack, a communications tool usually reserved for offices and corporate communications. I joined, and through a haze of embarrassment and anxiety, introduced myself in the introductions channel, only to be welcomed by people who were familiar with my work and glad that I was there. I found channels in the community for a variety of interests, from plant care to video games, and people I felt comfortable talking to and sharing my authentic stories with in a way I hadn't felt able to share up to that point. Some people had been in my industry for twice as long as I had, and others were just entering, but all of them had amazing thoughts and advice. There were people who called me out when I found myself piling onto other people's professional concerns with my personal distaste for someone, and people who came to my emotional rescue when I was feeling so down and out that I was ready to give up on my career entirely. That community quite literally saved my life, and I can't begin to thank them—the people who created it, run it on a daily basis, and participate in it—enough for that.

FOCUS ON YOUR IDENTITY

You may not be a journalist or even a person of color, but finding that kind of community space or even creating it for yourself is so incredibly important that I can't overstate how validating it is. I'm certain communities like this exist in a variety of fields, and if they don't, it might be time to grab some friends you can trust and make one. Virtually every branch of academia and science has a professional organization dedicated to sharing knowledge and research and generally just getting together with people you don't necessarily know or work with. And while those groups are helpful, they're often a seedbed for even more organizations dedicated to people who might be marginalized in those fields. For example, there might be groups that are all women, or all people of color, or all people with disabilities, and their mission is to discuss and share stories and strategies for success based on their identities. Don't let the broader world tell you that focusing on your identity like this is irrelevant to your work—instead, it's essential. Sure, it's essential for your career success to meet and network with other people who work in the same field and share ideas and personal stories, but it's also essential for your mental health to know that you're not alone, you're not isolated, and you don't have to feel like you are.

All that work eventually led me to realize that the *Times* wasn't my dream job after all and that I had talents and experience to be a superstar anywhere, but especially somewhere else. So I made the smart decision to leave what many would consider an incredible job for one where I am respected and challenged and able to work on things I love.

Sound familiar? If you've tried working around the problem, explored getting on a different team, or maybe tried mentally mollifying a bad situation by getting paid more, then you might understand. Or maybe you've even tried working with HR to find out how you could correct the marginalization you're experiencing at work. But none of it has worked.

If it's all too much, that's fine. It might be time to take your credentials, your diary, your list of accomplishments, and all the skills you've picked up just trying to survive in a workplace where you've been marginalized and put them to better use elsewhere. And that's something worth remembering, too: Your skills and talents are valuable. If you're worried you'll never find another job, don't worry; you will. And think less about finding another job and more about how you deserve a better job. Besides, if you want to really be productive, wouldn't you get more done, more work that matters (and matters to you) done, and have the opportunity to really bring your skills to bear on things that you're actually passionate about if you didn't have to deal with being sidelined and marginalized and wondering how you can be productive and succeed in spite of it?

But before I tell you to just go ahead and quit, let's look at some of the situations where it might be worthwhile to try to stick it out. For help, I turned to an old friend: Hannah Morgan, job search strategist and well-known career coach, who helped me a great deal when I wrote about office culture and job-related tips at *Lifehacker* and again at the *Times*.

DON'T FORGET THAT ALL JOBS
HAVE A LEARNING CURVE

Morgan reminded me that there's a learning curve at any job, so don't assume that leaving one place and joining another is automatically going to solve all the issues you've struggled with so far. "Here's what you should understand," she told me. "You owe it to yourself to be content with your work. There's a learning curve with every job. That could be three months or longer. So before you give up, ask yourself what it would take to make the situation better. Would you feel more comfortable if you knew how to solve work problems? Would you feel less stressed if you had someone you could ask for help or advice? If the hours are long or you don't have time to take care of your personal needs, ask yourself if this is the company culture or a high level of perfection you've set for yourself."

FIND A WORK BUDDY

Morgan also suggested that you find a colleague you trust, maybe someone who could be your "work buddy" or someone in one of the ERGs mentioned earlier, if these groups are available at your job. I remember when I had the privilege of meeting with the legendary Sam Sifton, the *New York Times* food editor and all-around amazing person. I asked him about his long career there and what it took to stick around for so long and do so many things. He told me that it was really just about flexibility, a willingness to do whatever comes your way when you have to do it, always keeping your eye on the next opportunity to do what you really want to do, and turning the work you have to do right now into work that you really love doing.

It is great advice, and I wish I had gotten to talk with Sifton more when I was at the *Times*. Maybe things would have worked out differently. "You don't necessarily need your boss's permission to seek out an informal mentor or work buddy," Morgan told me. Everyone should have a work buddy or someone who's been at the company for a long time and who knows the ins and outs of management and the winds that blow through the company as a whole, especially if that company is a large one, with teams and departments responsible for vastly different things. The work buddy can also help you figure out if your problems are surmountable or not.

BEFORE YOU MAKE ANY MOVE, IDENTIFY THE SOURCE OF THE PROBLEM

Depending on the situation you're facing at work, you may be able to sidestep it and find some solace elsewhere without having to update your résumé and get your best interview clothes dry-cleaned. Before you do anything, ask yourself these three questions.

Is the Problem Your Manager?

The old saying "People don't leave jobs; they leave bosses" is only partly true, but it's true enough that the first question you have to contend with is whether your manager is, or is part of, the problem you're facing. If you're being assigned office housework endlessly, with no opportunity to pick up glamour work, and when you do speak up for yourself, your manager shoots you down or listens to your concerns but never does anything about them, then the issue may be your boss. In that case, you might solve the issue by switching bosses if you can.

For example, this might be a good situation for moving to another team in your same company or applying for a position in your company where internal candidates may get preferred consideration. You never know; the problem might wind up being an opportunity in disguise.

Is the Problem Your Team?

If the issue you're facing is because of a troublesome coworker (or group of coworkers) on your team or at your company, you have a slightly more difficult issue to reckon with. Ask yourself how closely you deal with the person who's marginalizing you. Do they exclude you from meetings that they attend in your stead, or do they actively tell other people to work with them instead of with you? The difference might mean that you can't escape their influence if you switch teams, and if your manager isn't willing to help when both you and this person are peers on the same team, there's no reason to believe that the manager will step in when you're on a different one. Similarly, you don't know if this colleague's influence extends to others at your organization, so you still may have to watch your back, even if you leave a problematic person—or problematic office clique—behind. In a lot of ways, being marginalized by peers is worse than being sidelined by managers, because peers have more insidious ways to make your life difficult and back channels to reinforce how much they want you on the sidelines.

Is the Problem the Culture at Work?

That brings me to the third and final question to ask: Maybe what's really marginalizing you isn't so much a specific person, a bad boss, or even a combination of the two, but these things combined with a toxic culture at work. Your problem is not due to any single person, be it a bad boss or an obnoxious colleague, but the cumulative effect of many people in a workplace either creating the marginalization, ignoring it, or even denying that it exists. People in that culture may dance around the toxicity, they may point fingers at others and claim how bad someone else is compared with how they are, and they may even perpetuate the cycle of backstabbing office politics by claiming that someone else was the first to cause offense. But at the end of the day, the culture is what it is, and it determines how far you'll rise and how much you'll succeed, regardless of your best efforts.

This is something that took me a long time to understand. In several of my jobs in journalism, I worked in environments that called themselves "high pressure" and "competitive." But not all high-pressure and competitive work environments are the same. At one publication, different teams playfully (sometimes too playfully) competed with one another for the biggest version of the same story, the best overall read, or the top of the leaderboard on a given day. At another high-pressure and competitive environment, every word needed to be justified, every assertion that didn't match up with someone else's expectation needed an email thread, and competition came in the form of people trying to undermine your work, steal your sources and writers, and otherwise quash your projects and plans. One environment was where someone like me, who isn't particularly interested in the nuances of office politics, could succeed. The other was a swamp, an environment where I knew I was doing important work but where it was impossible to feel good about any of it because the fight to get anything done was so hard that every win felt like a Pyrrhic victory.

If it is time to leave, know that you won't be starting from scratch. As Morgan said to me, "everything you learn about yourself, what you need from work, and how to handle a bad situation are valuable lessons you'll take with you and will make you wiser and more capable in the future."

IT'S NOT ON YOU TO FIX SYSTEMIC ISSUES

Whether you're being marginalized in particular because of your race, your gender, your religion, your age, your ability level, or anything else, keep this one truism in mind: *It's not your job to fix a workplace's systemic discrimination issues.* Especially if you're in a toxic environment and are a victim of those issues, it's not your job. Sure, you can try to work around individuals, and you can try to massage well-meaning but poor managers into action. You can even try to sidestep larger issues that might be systemic in your organization and that you have no control over. But what you can't do—and can't be expected to do—is fix them. And too often, people in marginalized groups come into workplaces hoping that finding some community and camaraderie with their coworkers will shield them from the workplace's systemic issues. Unfortunately, they soon learn that the ERGs they join and the unions they help found are forced by management (and others with no stake in the marginalization, of course) to wrangle with the company's toxicity themselves. It shouldn't be on a company's ERG for disabled workers to try to force management to make a more accessible workplace, but it often is, and managers and able-bodied employees alike won't do anything until the right people speak up about it. When I discussed the dichotomy of trying, as a marginalized person, to do your best work and work around people who may not be aware of their own privilege, and while simultaneously understanding that it's not your responsibility to make a company stop being racist, Ruchika Tulshyan agreed. "My fervent belief is all of us, especially biased managers, can change and grow, but it takes intention," she said. "I grew up in a country where I did not see or even interact with a Black American person in my early years. My early influences were shaped by harmful (Western) media portrayals of Black people, and when I immigrated to the UK first and then the US, it was abundantly clear that the racist ideas I had been conditioned to believe were unacceptable and harmful. It takes intention and hard work to undo that. So while we all have social baggage, I refuse to accept that a white person can't change to become more inclusive and practice antiracism. In fact, it is a hundred percent possible and should be expected of every single person in our society."

Adam Grant agreed, and when we were talking about how to communicate how busy you are, he brought up the issue of collective responsibility. "It should not be an individual's responsibility, especially if you're a person of color. I think this is the organization's problem to figure out how to measure your contribution, not whether you're busy or not. I think it's a structural and cultural problem, not an individual problem, but to your point, we can't just sit around waiting until we fix all the broken systems and organizations that hold people of color back."

Both he and Tulshyan are right, and those are battles you should have the right to choose to fight, on your own terms, not battles you're forced to fight just to survive in a workplace. When I was the only Black editor in chief of a Gawker Media publication, I didn't ask to suddenly have to reckon with the company's racial issues, and I didn't ask to essentially be *the* representative of Black people when our company was subsequently acquired. That baggage came with me, regardless of what I wanted, but at the end of the day, it wasn't on me to fix management's issues with anti-Blackness, nor did I get the opportunity. When I joined the *New York Times*, I didn't immediately ask to be part of a conversation to steer diversity in the newsroom in the right direction and to further diversify the bylines and sources that appeared in the paper. But eventually I became part of these conversations, because I chose to engage in them, hire contributors whose voices weren't represented in the paper, and let them air perspectives they may not otherwise have had an opportunity to share. I chose to be a part of that conversation, and in some ways, I paid the price for it, although I don't regret it.

In fact, a study published in the *Academy of Management Journal* pointed out that women and nonwhite executives who often stand up for diversity and equity in their workplaces wind up being punished for their efforts, either through microaggressions or otherwise, when it comes to performance reviews from their bosses.[1] The study continued that the only people who were actually rewarded for their diversity and inclusion efforts were white men, which says a lot by itself. And I can echo that experience.

You should go into all those scenarios with eyes wide open, knowing that even though you're bringing along baggage that you didn't pack and had no intention of carrying, it's still not your job to fix people's mindsets about who you are and what you're capable of unless you choose to. What's more, you don't owe it to yourself or anyone else to go out on a limb to prove that you and people like you are capable of anything. If someone doesn't already know that or believe it, your sacrificing your mental health and stability won't do it—and even if it did, it wouldn't be worth it.

TAKE YOUR SKILLS WITH YOU

If the environment is too much to bear, or you've tried the tips I've mentioned, or you've already decided that it's time to just go, don't just quit. I know, it might feel refreshing or even like sweet revenge to walk in one day and tell the manager who never helped you to shove it. And there's a time and a place for that, trust me, but if things have gotten to that point, you probably don't need my advice. More power to you.

If it hasn't gotten to that point, though, or you still need to pay the bills before you find something new, then make your moves in silence. That's perhaps my best job search advice: Move quickly, move quietly, and move with intention.

MAKE SURE YOU HAVE A NEW JOB
BEFORE QUITTING YOUR OLD JOB

I asked Morgan for more tips on getting out of Dodge without burning your bridges. She agreed that moving in silence and with intention is key, and she added that it's incredibly important to make sure you have a job, if you can do so, before you leave your current job, even if your current job is making you miserable.

"It will be more work, and you may feel like you don't have the mental energy to job search while in a job you hate, but here's why you want to," she told me. "Looking for a new job when you are unemployed is stressful. You worry about money. You worry about not finding a job soon enough. You worry that people will wonder why you left. You have a bit more confidence and less fear and stress when you search for a job while employed. Set a deadline for a date you want to leave so there's hope and a light at the end of the tunnel."

In a marketplace that claims to prize diversity but whose hiring numbers and diversity reports don't bear that out, and in an environment where hiring managers are always claiming they want to do better rather than actually fix the pay, racial, age, and gender disparities on their teams, you need to advocate for yourself first. Take your time finding an opportunity worth grabbing instead of just bailing and then leaping at the first new opportunity you encounter. Going too quickly causes many people to fall into a cycle of moving from one toxic environment to the next, trading out a bad boss for a toxic teammate, and a toxic teammate for being underpaid.

WRITE DOWN EVERYTHING YOU HATE ABOUT YOUR JOB

When I asked Morgan what job seekers can do to make sure they don't fall into a toxic workplace again, she was emphatic. "Everyone has a different tolerance for toxic work environments. What triggers one person may not trigger you. So it's important to write down all the things you hated about your last job: how your boss communicated, rules and policies, camaraderie on the team, and other work culture characteristics." If you haven't already done so, now is a great time to pull thoughts from your work diary. Ideally you'll have a lot of that information in it, but if you're ready to leave and haven't had a chance to start such a diary, now is a good time to get into the habit. Plus, getting all these thoughts on paper prepares you for your search, so you can try to avoid companies that seem a little too much like the one you're leaving.

"During the interview process," Morgan said, "ask behavior-based questions to understand how things work there. For example, if you don't like being micromanaged, don't ask the interviewer if they are a micromanager or how they manage. Instead, ask a situational question like 'Tell me about how you like to communicate with your team' or 'Can you give me an example of how you communicate work deadlines?'"

Morgan also suggested doing a little intelligence work. See if you can find people on LinkedIn who worked at that company you're interested in and check the company's reviews on Glassdoor and other sites where employees can air their grievances about their employers. If you can talk to someone directly, ask them what they liked and disliked about working there, what they heard about the other teams in the organization, and so on. You'll probably get a variety of answers, but at least you'll have something to go on. Similarly, when you read sites like Glassdoor, keep in mind that as with any review site, people are more inclined to use them to complain and share stories of how they were poorly treated than they are to share positive experiences. So take the comments with the appropriate grain of salt. Just watch out for anything that looks systemic or any common threads across reviews, such as issues of pay, poor management or leadership, or—most relevant to marginalized employees—unfair treatment that goes unaddressed in the workplace.

So what about starting that new job when you find it? How do you avoid the sinking suspicion that as soon as the honeymoon glamour has passed after your first few weeks or months, the cracks will start to show and you'll hate your new job as much as you hated your last one? Morgan said that some of it is just how the nature of our always-on, always-hustling work culture grinds us down, and some of it is a self-fulfilling prophecy. "Starting a new job is also a chance for you to reinvent yourself," she told me. "What can you do to be the best version of yourself? What bad habits can you drop (we all have them)? Starting a new job with a new set of people is a clean slate. It's also a chance to build some healthy new habits."

HOW TO AVOID MOVING TO YET ANOTHER TERRIBLE JOB

Activate your network first. When I was at *Lifehacker,* I wrote an article about a technique called "the layoff test."[2] In short, think about who you would call if you were laid off from your current job tomorrow: friends, former colleagues, old managers you're in good standing with, people you might want as a reference. If you can't think of anyone, it's time to start building those connections now, before you need them. And if you *can* think of people but haven't spoken to them in a while, now might be a good time, before you really need them, to get in touch and catch up to see how their professional lives are coming along and to let them know how you're doing. Then, when it's time to make a move, you can reach out again and say, "Hey, I think I might be looking for new opportunities. Do you have any leads?"

Use the experience you've gained. Remember all that talk about finding the productivity method that works for you and about keeping a work diary so you have a written record of your wins, your challenges, and even the small things that happened to you, both positive and negative, at work? Now is the time to use all the information you've collected. Build your résumé with all those wins, especially the biggest ones. Include the projects you championed and the glamour work you tackled. Even add the housework, especially since, if you were stuck with it, you were the only one who was capable of doing it well. If you scheduled all the meetings, it's fair to say that you "juggled multiple priorities and made sure that regular check-ins with stakeholders were scheduled and managed," for example. Take all those wins and all that experience and use it to your best revenge: getting a better job that will treat you with respect and dignity.

Grab your data. This recommendation is a little controversial, and many organizations prohibit you from downloading emails, contacts, and other work-related information before you leave a job. But they don't stop you from sending some of your closest colleagues, sources, clients, or other people you work with a quick email to say, "Hey, if you ever need to reach me, just in case, here's my phone number and personal email address." Even if you can't take a lot of your data with you, you *can* take relationships, and those are way more important. If you can take files that document some of the great work you've done, grab them, along with awards you've earned or anything else that has personal or professional significance for you. Ask the IT folks what their policies are and if they can help you back stuff up. Better to do it now than on your last day.

Don't burn your bridges. You may be tempted to get everything off your chest in your exit interview with HR. Don't. It's just not worth it. That's if you even get an interview. On their way out, marginalized folks seldom get the kind of HR attention that other employees do. But if you do, don't burn your bridges. You may feel the urge to tell HR all about your marginalization—the manager who didn't help, the colleagues who harassed you, and so on—but unless you think anything will seriously come of it, keep your stories to your personal whisper networks and don't say anything that may come back to haunt you in a professional or even a legal capacity.[3] Remember, you don't owe your soon-to-be-former employer any intel on what's broken in the company culture.[4] The company can figure it out after you're gone.

Take a break, and don't feel guilty about it. Finally, and perhaps most important, don't feel guilty about leaving your company at all. This isn't on you. Jenny Foss, writing for career-advice website The Muse, explained that there are four primary reasons you shouldn't feel guilty about leaving your job. First, professionals are expected to grow and evolve and move on to new opportunities. If someone else were doing it, you might miss them, but you wouldn't feel bad, right? Second, if the tables were turned, the company would cut you loose without thinking twice about it. You know how layoffs can be. Third, if you stay and remain miserable out of some sense of guilt over what you'd leave behind if you left, you're not doing anyone any favors, including yourself. And fourth, she explained that if you let it, guilt will take the joy out of your final two weeks at a job, when you should be celebrating your move and promising to stay in touch with colleagues turned friends. Add them to your professional network instead, as I recommended in the first step in this section. Stay in touch with them, and you'll be fine. And give yourself a little time to recuperate between jobs. Don't rush from one job to the next, unless you must do so to keep the bills paid.

HOW TO GET OFF TO A PRODUCTIVE START

Morgan offered a few suggestions for your first few days in your new job as well. She mentioned this important question: "Who are the important people you should know (and who should know you) in the company?" In the newsroom, there was no real official onboarding process for me. Don't get me wrong, I met wonderful people those first few days, including the administrative team members who made sure I had a brand-new laptop on my first day and the people who helped me figure out where I should sit and how to navigate the building. But aside from a quick HR session to go over employee benefits, there was no real training. Instead, I wound up spending a few dozen hours sitting with an administrator of the *New York Times* publishing system, learning the technical ins and outs of publishing a story for the website. All of it was stuff that, looking back, was more news assistant work than senior editor work, but I was just happy to have something to do other than what I was doing at that point—sitting at my desk reading every story that went live so I could get a feel for the voice and editing style. Well, that and wondering when I'd be allowed to commission, edit, and publish stories of my own. (And, ironically, when I did finally get the right to do that, a teammate who had a long reputation for trying to marginalize me threw a fit and went to my manager to complain about my getting the opportunity to do the job they'd hired me to do. This should give you insight into what I was up against. And when he wasn't reprimanded for that behavior, the lack of action should have told me everything I needed to know about our management.)

But one thing that my manager did that I'm eternally grateful for was initially setting up meetings with other senior editors and newsroom leaders so I could get the lay of the land and meet people I could potentially work with. That was how I made friends in the newsroom nice and early, and I'd recommend it to anyone starting a new job, if possible—reach out early on to people you may wind up working with, even if you don't think you'll work with them regularly.

THERE ARE OTHER WAYS TO FEEL FULFILLED; JUST GO

Finally, a reminder to all of us in the workplace—especially marginalized folks—that the entire workforce isn't the same as the awful place you're at, or the place you may have been, or the place that inspired you to pick up this book. Yes, sometimes it's worth plugging away or switching teams and staying with a company that's rich with opportunity but perhaps on a team that's far from a problematic person or manager. Yes, sometimes it's worth finding your tribe at an office and joining a team that will not only protect and insulate you from the bad actors elsewhere but also elevate your work. I've had the privilege of working on all those types of teams, in various fields.

However, other times it's more prudent to seek out a new opportunity elsewhere, at a company more committed to a diverse workplace or an inclusive team or at a place that may even give you more of the opportunities you deserve. If you have in place a rock-solid productivity system that works best for the way you work, if you're armed with data about how you've worked in the past and your capabilities, and if you're self-aware enough to know when systemic problems are working against you (as opposed to you working against yourself), then you'll thrive in any of those places. And that's what I did. I broke ranks and left an extremely prestigious institution. But really, I was leaving a toxic environment, not the institution, which I still believe does important work and has many talented people struggling with their own marginalization every day. I fled this situation to enjoy both an opportunity that nourishes me and a team that supports me in a way I had forgotten existed, and I sleep much better at night. And if or when this job does stop giving me what I need and want, I'll move on again, remembering these good times but without reservation about what I'm leaving behind.

Back in 2015, I wrote an article for *Lifehacker* headlined "The Company You Work for Is Not Your Friend."[5] I maintain that this is the truth and has always been the truth. The piece was so successful not because I was imparting something particularly new, but because I had crystallized the sentiment into something that rolls off the tongue so easily. Your employer is just that, an employer. Your company calls the unit that handles employee issues its *human resources department* for a reason—you're a resource. Sure, you're also a person, a human being with thoughts and feelings and needs, but our system of work usually doesn't factor in the personal part of you unless you're lucky enough to work for an employer that cares about such things in an honest and transparent way. When I was in business school, I learned that there's a reason we referred to employees as *human capital*. In many ways, even skilled workers with advanced degrees or masters of their trades are often viewed as assets to a company, some employees worth more than others, but none of them absolutely irreplaceable. So don't give your employer some bit of your heart and soul unless—and this is a strong *unless*—you have some actual stake in the game. Maybe you're one of the lucky folks who work for a family-owned business and everyone really does look out for each other. That's great. Maybe you work for a company whose CEO will take a pay cut to make sure the staff doesn't have to lay anyone off or you work where there's a union ready to fight for your benefits and raises. Good for you! But remember, there's no rule that says you need to put up with being marginalized, discriminated against, or otherwise made to feel less than the superstar you can be with the right opportunities at work.

The door is always there, and you're free to open it, walk through it, and never look back.

ACKNOWLEDGMENTS

This book wouldn't have been possible without the guidance and support of many, many people. More people than I can name, but let's give it a shot. First, all my thanks to Ruchika Tulshyan for her unending support, expertise, and encouragement, not just with this book, but with the *New York Times* article that laid the groundwork for this book. Her writing on the differences between office "housework" and "glamour work," along with the research that Joan C. Williams has done on the same topic—and that she so kindly shared with me for this book—gave me an opportunity to see my experiences as systemic injustices and not individual failures. Their work gave me the freedom and flexibility to start thinking of these problems as things I could solve, for myself and for others.

This book also wouldn't be possible without the team at Rodale and Random House working behind the scenes to bring this to your hands. My editor, Matthew Benjamin, whose enthusiasm for this book kept me going, and whose email asking if I wanted to talk about turning my story into a book landed in my spam folder accidentally (check your spam folder, friends!). My literary agent, William LoTurco, who met a very nervous me for lunch and explained over a very heavily dressed Caesar salad that this story could do real good for people who need it, and that I was absolutely the person to tell it. Patricia Boyd, the copy editor who massaged my many overly long sentences and wordy paragraphs into digestible text.

Speaking of research, special thanks to the journalists, authors, and scientists who took time to speak with me and share their insight and expertise for this book. In addition to Ruchika and Joan, thank you to: Adam Grant, whose work has long since been an inspiration to me and whose assistance (and not to mention friendship) was invaluable to quantifying the issues I outline in the book. Charles Duhigg, my productivity partner in crime and an incredible mentor. David Cadavy, whose insight on productivity reinforced the fact that we're in the business of helping people use their time better, not use it in the service of tools or apps. Derald Wing Sue, whose research on microaggressions gave language to something marginalized people have always felt. Emma Carew Grovum, who donated not only great suggestions for how to value your own work, but also the rule I used to title that chapter. Hannah Morgan, the career coach who's never led me wrong. Hahna Yoon, whose work with me at the *Times* highlighted how much we have in common (and for the amazing snacks). Katherine Crowley and Kathi Elster, whose consulting work is changing workplaces and changing lives (including mine, thanks to their expertise). Kevin Nadal, for his microaggression response handbook, which I personally live by. Kristin Wong, for her expertise on money matters and on book-writing, but, more important, for her enduring friendship. Meghan French Dunbar, who was entirely more helpful than she thought (or thinks) she was. Melanie Pinola, an amazing writer and an incredible friend. Saadia Muzzafar, whose work on behalf of underrepresented people in tech spaces has always been an inspiration. And Vivek Haldar, the Google developer who popularized the phrase "productivity porn" and took time to chat with me about it.

ACKNOWLEDGMENTS

This book also wouldn't be possible without the many, many people personally who keep my emotional tanks fueled and my little ship of creativity ready to sail. My mother, Olga Henry, who taught me how to chart my own course in everything that I do, and my father, Nelson Henry, who showed me how to navigate that course; they are proud of my every step. Jack Wallace, the one person on this earth who knows me better than anyone else and has never once stopped loving me and pushing me toward greatness. Thank you, I love you. Andre Thomas, who helped me break down my own mental walls and barriers, challenged me to do right by myself, and called me out on my own bullshit.

Annalee Newitz, my comrade in arms, book accountability buddy, and incredible, inspiring friend. Kenneth Rosen, you and I both deserved better, and I'm glad we both got it. Caroline Que, who helped encourage me to write this book when I didn't feel empowered to do so. To my *Lifehacker* refugee squad: Adam Pash, Whitson Gordon, Adam Dachis, Eric Ravenscraft, Thorin Klosowski, Andy Orin, Joshua Rivera, Claire Lower, and Beth Skwarecki: May your careers be long and your pageviews be many. Lacey Donohue, for her leadership, advice, and (I didn't forget!) emotional labor. Kendra Pierre-Louis, for ripping the wool from my eyes several times over. Karen Ho, for her insight, her friendship, and entirely too many good Goodwill auctions. Tessa Miller, for reminding me every day that we make the beautiful things in this world, we don't wait for them to come to us. Tim Pumplin, my best friend for decades upon decades. Also, my undying love and thanks to the people whose friendship and love saved me during some pretty difficult times: Ree, for reaching back when I reached out and it turning into a friendship that I don't have words to express (and I'm an editor). Kayla, for transcending our boundaries and being an amazing, compassionate friend. Ruby, for being my New York fam and the most inspiring, entertaining gremlin I've ever had the privilege of being friends with. Ruggs, for sharing a pop culture brain cell with me. Lupine, for warmth and laughter that's infectious even on my dark days. And Mark, who showed me that you know, I don't have to be alone around these parts.

I'm especially grateful to everyone in Journalists of Color who inspired me to write this book, told me it was important, and even set up bots and other reminders to make sure I did it. Special shout-out to my JOC Dungeons & Dragons group, who would get me inspired to write and edit after hours of goblin slaying and casting Animal Friendship. And thank you, last but not least, to the army of TikTok and Instagram animals and memes that soothe my weary soul.

NOTES

RULE 1

1. Alan Henry, "How to Succeed When You're Marginalized or Discriminated Against at Work," *New York Times*, October 6, 2019, www.nytimes.com/2019/10/01/smarter-living/ productivity-without-privilege-discrimination-work.html.

2. For a discussion of white people's lack of Black friends, see Daniel Cox, Juhem Navarro-Rivera, and Robert P. Jones, "Race, Religion, and Political Affiliation of Americans' Core Social Networks," PRRI (Public Religion Research Institute), August 3, 2016, www.prri.org/research/poll-race-religion -politics-americans-social-networks.

RULE 2

1. Derald Wing Sue, "Microaggression: More Than Just Race," UUA (Unitarian Universalist Association), www.uua.org/files/ pdf/m/microaggressions_by_derald_wing_sue_ph.d._.pdf, accessed March 11, 2021.

2. Hahna Yoon, "How to Respond to Microaggressions," *New York Times*, March 3, 2020, www.nytimes.com/2020/03/03/smarter -living/how-to-respond-to-microaggressions.html.

3. Kevin L. Nadal, "A Guide to Responding to Microaggressions—Asian Americans," http://arks.princeton.edu/ark:/88435/dsp01rv042w977. Accessed August 15, 2021.

4. Gina Torino, "How Racism and Microaggressions Lead to Worse Health," *Center for Health Journalism*, November 10, 2017, https://centerforhealthjournalism.org/2017/11/08/how-racism-and-microaggressions-lead-worse-health.

5. Margaret T. Hicken, Hedwig Lee, Jeffrey Morenoff, James S. House, and David R. Williams, "Racial/Ethnic Disparities in Hypertension Prevalence: Reconsidering the Role of Chronic Stress," *American Journal of Public Health* 104, no. 1 (2014): 117–123, www.ncbi.nlm.nih.gov/pmc/articles/PMC3910029.

6. Victoria M. O'Keefe, LaRicka R. Wingate, Ashley B. Cole, David W. Hollingsworth, and Raymond P. Tucker, "Seemingly Harmless Racial Communications Are Not So Harmless: Racial Microaggressions Lead to Suicidal Ideation by Way of Depression Symptoms," *Suicide and Life Threatening Behavior* 45, no. 5 (2015): 567–576, https://pubmed.ncbi.nlm.nih.gov/25556819.

7. Jay Smooth, "How to Tell Someone They Sound Racist," YouTube video, July 21, 2008, www.youtube.com/watch?v=b0Ti-gkJiXc.

RULE 3

1. Jennifer J. Freyd, "What is DARVO?," 2021, https://dynamic.uoregon.edu/jjf/defineDARVO.html, accessed March 16, 2021.

RULE 4

1. Gillian B. White, "Black Workers Really Do Need to Be Twice as Good," *Atlantic*, October 7, 2015.

RULE 5

1. Ruchika Tulshyan, "Women of Color Get Asked to Do More 'Office Housework.' Here's How They Can Say No," *Harvard Business Review*, April 6, 2018, https://hbr.org/2018/04/women-of-color-get-asked-to-do-more-office-housework-heres-how-they-can-say-no.

2. Joan C. Williams and Marina Multhaup, "For Women and Minorities to Get Ahead, Managers Must Assign Work Fairly," *Harvard Business Review*, March 5, 2018, https://hbr.org/2018/03/for-women-and-minorities-to-get-ahead-managers-must-assign-work-fairly.

RULE 6

1. Ashleigh Shelby Rosette, Geoffrey J. Leonardelli, and Katherine W. Phillips, "The White Standard: Racial Bias in Leader Categorization," *Journal of Applied Psychology* 93, no. 4 (2008): 758–777, https://pubmed.ncbi.nlm.nih.gov/18642982.

RULE 8

1. Tim Kreider, "The 'Busy' Trap," *New York Times*, June 30, 2012, https://opinionator.blogs.nytimes.com/2012/06/30/the-busy-trap.

2. Matt Heinz, "An Introduction to Productivity Porn: How to Be Lazy, Productive & Successful," *GeekWire*, February 12, 2012,

www.geekwire.com/2012/introduction-productivity-porn-lazy
-productive-successful.

3. For a discussion of Maslow's hierarchy, see Saul McLeod,
"Maslow's Hierarchy of Needs," *Simply Psychology,*
December 29, 2020, www.simplypsychology.org/maslow.html.

RULE 9

1. Melanie Pinola, "Work Only Your 'Good Hours' to Become
More Productive," *Lifehacker,* June 9, 2011, https://lifehacker
.com/work-only-your-good-hours-to-become-more-productive
-5810290.

2. Melanie Pinola, "Take More Breaks, Get More Done,"
Lifehacker, June 20, 2012, https://lifehacker.com/take-more-
breaks-get-more-done-5919897.

3. Adam Grant was referring to this research: David R. Hekman,
Stefanie K. Johnson, Maw-Der Foo, and Wei Yang, "Does
Diversity-Valuing Behavior Result in Diminished Performance
Ratings for Non-White and Female Leaders?" *Academy of
Management Journal* 60, no. 2 (2016): 771–797, https://journals
.aom.org/doi/abs/10.5465/amj.2014.0538.

RULE 10

1. Alan Henry, "The Weekly Review: How One Hour Can Save
You a Week's Worth of Hassle and Headaches," *Lifehacker,* May
9, 2012, https://lifehacker.com/the-weekly-review-how-one-
hour-can-save-you-a-week-s-w-5908816.

RULE 12

1. "How to Succeed When You're Marginalized or Discriminated Against at Work," October 6, 2019, https://www.nytimes.com/2019/10/01/smarter-living/productivity-without-privilege-discrimination-work.html. Accessed 22 Mar. 2021.

2. Glen Stansberry, "5 Reasons to Keep a Work Diary," American Express, June 28, 2011, www.americanexpress.com/en-us/business/trends-and-insights/articles/5-reasons-to-keep-a-work-diary.

RULE 13

1. Alan Henry, "How to Stay Productive When the World Is on Fire," *Wired*, July 22, 2020, www.wired.com/story/productivity-tips-coronavirus-work-from-home.

2. Jason Chen, "The Comfort Principle: Spend Money Where You Spend Your Time," *Lifehacker*, November 7, 2011, https://lifehacker.com/the-comfort-principle-spend-money-where-you-spend-your-5857142.

RULE 14

1. For US data, see US Bureau of Labor Statistics, "Usual Weekly Earnings of Wage and Salary Workers: First Quarter 2021," news release, April 16, 2021, www.bls.gov/news.release/pdf/wkyeng.pdf.

2. Janelle Jones, "5 Facts About the State of the Gender Pay Gap," US Department of Labor Blog, March 19, 2021, https://blog.dol.gov/2021/03/19/5-facts-about-the-state-of-the-gender-pay-gap.

3. "The Racial Wage Gap Persists in 2020," PayScale, www
.payscale.com/data/racial-wage-gap, accessed July 10, 2021;
Amy Stewart, "Black Women Deserve Equal Pay," PayScale,
August 13, 2020, www.payscale.com/compensation-today/
2020/08/black-women-equal-pay-2020.

4. Hengchen Dai, Xiaoyang Long, and Dennis Zhang, "Wage
Transparency, Negotiation, and Reference-Dependent Utility,"
SSRN, March 16, 2021, https://papers.ssrn.com/sol3/papers
.cfm?abstract_id=3805864.

5. "'Bargaining While Black' May Lead to Lower Salaries,"
American Psychological Association, November 7, 2018, www
.apa.org/news/press/releases/2018/11/bargaining-black.

6. Patti Phillips, "Zone of Possibility," TEDx Talks, YouTube
video, April 20, 2015, www.youtube.com/watch?v=
ALcHyVIcx00.

RULE 15

1. David R. Hekman, Stefanie K. Johnson, Maw-Der Foo, and
Wei Yang, "Does Diversity-Valuing Behavior Result in
Diminished Performance Ratings for Non-White and Female
Leaders?," *Academy of Management Journal* 60 no. 2 (2016): 771–
797, https://journals.aom.org/doi/abs/10.5465/amj.2014.0538;
Elizabeth Lock, "Women, Nonwhite Execs Promote Diversity
to Their Own Detriment, Says CU-Boulder Study," *CU Boulder
Today,* April 11, 2016, www.colorado.edu/today/2016/04/11/
women-nonwhite-execs-promote-diversity-their-own-detriment
-says-cu-boulder-study.

2. Alan Henry, "Use the 'Layoff Test' to Build Your Professional Network," *Lifehacker*, December 27, 2012, https://lifehacker.com/use-the-layoff-test-to-build-your-professional-networ-5971451.

3. Alan Henry, "How Honest Should I Be in My Exit Interview?," *Lifehacker*, February 27, 2012, https://lifehacker.com/how-honest-should-i-be-in-my-exit-interview-5888549.

4. Robbie Abed, "Don't Lie on Your Resume, but Lie Like Hell During Your Exit Interview," *Lifehacker*, October 16, 2012, https://lifehacker.com/dont-lie-on-your-resume-but-lie-like-hell-during-your-5952185.

5. Alan Henry, "The Company You Work for Is Not Your Friend," *Lifehacker*, March 18, 2015, https://lifehacker.com/the-company-you-work-for-is-not-your-friend-1692113529.

INDEX

ABOUT THE AUTHOR

Alan Henry is a journalist and editor who covers technology and productivity, and their intersection with our lives and culture. He's written and edited stories that help readers figure out the best apps to organize their lives, as well as the best ways to organize a kitchen or take charge of their own health or career. He is currently the senior editor for service journalism at *Wired*, where he writes and commissions stories that help readers make better use of their technology and embrace a healthier relationship with it in their lives. He also oversees *Wired* Games, the team at *Wired* covering video games, gaming culture, and gaming as a cultural force. He was previously the smarter living editor at the *New York Times* and before that the editor in chief of the productivity and lifestyle blog *Lifehacker*. He has bachelor's degrees in physics and astronomy and a master's in business administration.